# Injustices of a Poetic Soul

*For Every Woman's Woes There is an Untold Story*

By

ISABELLA M.

authorHOUSE®

*AuthorHouse™*
*1663 Liberty Drive, Suite 200*
*Bloomington, IN 47403*
*www.authorhouse.com*
*Phone: 1-800-839-8640*

*First published by AuthorHouse 5/28/2008*

*ISBN: 978-1-4343-7814-9 (sc)*

*Library of Congress Control Number: 2008904819*

*Printed in the United States of America*
*Bloomington, Indiana*

*This book is printed on acid-free paper.*

# Dedication

I dedicate this book to my five saviors, EE, Jahjah, Pooty, Nini, and Pooda. Without you there is no me, but without me, there would not be you. You are everything to me and I am everything to you. That is why we complete each other. I love you all dearly and all of my success is because of you. I strived to make everything happen that we wanted and needed; so that you will have more to offer your children then I did mine. The cycle of a positive movement must continue through you, and the negative cycle ends through me! Without you all in my life, I would not be anything but perhaps a stupid drunk, a drug addict, or maybe I would have ended my pain years ago, but my children, you gave me life, taught me love, and made a real woman out of me. God bless you and thank you! I also would like to dedicate this book to life itself because life is hard to live and no matter how rich, poor, happy or unhappy you are life will bite you right in the ass when you are least expectant. Although you may be disappointed in some of the language that I have used to express myself, I am dedicating this book to you, too, grandfather, because it was your strength I valued. I also look up to you because you strived for greatness in your life and created a wonderful life for yourself. Thank you for being a positive role model in my life! Last, but not least, and never least, THANK YOU GOD FOR ALL THAT YOU HAVE GIVEN ME! I love you all! Peace.

*The photos in this book were taken by:*
*Iman Hughes and Janiyah Cobbs*

*Models are:*
*Isabella M. and Janiyah Cobbs*

# Title: You are

*Iman, you are a queen. You give meaning to my life.*
*Although it seems there are endless struggles and strife*
*You turn darkness into light, and sadness into glory.*
*You turn my nightmares into dreams and bring happy endings to my sad stories.*
*You are every mother's hope because you are so good to me.*
*You are every girl's envy because you are as beautiful as can be.*
*When the sky seems so gloomy, you bring me an inevitable smile.*
*No matter where you go, you will always be queen of the Nile.*
*Laughter and joy is what you bring into our home.*
*You are comfort to everyone and without you, we'd all feel alone.*
*You are trustworthy, honest; sometimes you are a pain in the ass.*
*You are my daughter from heaven, and that's all I could ask.*
*From the very first glance into your eyes, you took my breath away.*
*You are my priceless gem, and in my heart you will forever stay.*
*I love you!*

# *Lost*

## January 14, 2008

*I am lost without self-love.*
*I am lost without self-respect.*
*I am lost without confidence.*
*I am lost if it is God that I reject.*
*I am lost without my mind all together.*
*I am lost within myself forever.*
*My optimism gone, lost by pessimism.*
*Scared to live life because of my skepticism.*
*My apathy for myself is due to self-hate.*
*Continuous negativity, wondering is this fate?*
*I am lost because I don't know who I am.*
*I am lost because I did not have a plan.*
*Racism, sexism, we can all relate.*
*Our journey through slavery left us lost in a terrible state.*
*Our fears used against us, our strengths taken away*
*We are lost mentally, through mental slavery today.*
*Still locked up in chains but it is all in our minds*
*Divided as a people because we are living in hard times.*
*I am lost because my people are lost, we have no unity*
*Fighting one another, killing each other in our own community.*
*We are all lost because we want to be free*
*Unlock those mental chains, and so shall it be!*

# Introduction

## Does Anyone Care?

*Please tell me, does anyone care?*
*Untold stories of a single mother,*
*Unheard of abuse of a sister and brother.*
*These are the things that we ignore.*
*No one cares because no one saw*
*A woman's cry for help while being brutally raped*
*A young black man arrested for an eyewitnesses mistake.*
*These are the things that many don't care.*
*The story of the minority that goes through "deaf ears"*
*Stories told through generations of slaves' tears of pain*
*A hungry homeless family sleeping outside in a cold rain.*
*These are the struggles that many have faced.*
*The struggles of the said inferior, memories that cannot be erased.*
*Commercials telling lies about their fantasy schemes*
*False prophecies of a poor man's dreams.*
*These are the things we call propaganda.*
*Nothing but the whispers of a devil's scandal.*
*The sunset by the horizon, the bright stars of a beautiful night,*
*The laughter of a child running down the beach while flying his kite.*
*These are the things some wish they could see*
*As some would love to smell the sweet scent of nectar or to taste honey from*
*a bee.*
*A person can always hope and they can always pray*
*We only seek to fulfill our wants, but our needs we neglect everyday.*
*A man may take for granted the things you should value most*
*To live, taste, touch, hear or see is a gift, but we would rather treasure*
*materials and it is of that we will boast.*
*Material things are the things that someday shall perish*
*To a blind, deaf, or paralyzed man to have what we should value, they*
*would cherish.*
*Please tell me, DOES ANYONE CARE?*

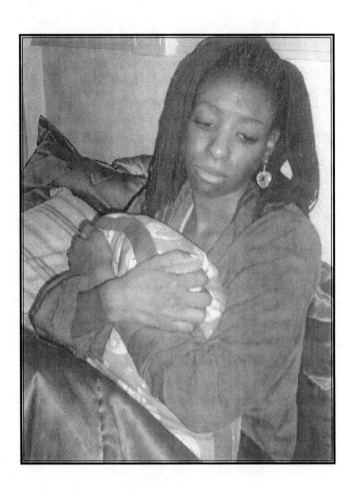

# Chapter 1: Sadness

## Injustices of a Poetic Soul

**July 18, 2007**

*Tight clothing, guns, drug dealing, and abuse*
*Mental Anguish, pain, disease, famine, and prejudice.*
*All have been a part of our lives*
*Caught in a web of deceitful lies.*
*Enslavement in our past, drug abuse to cope*
*Unity is no longer; our lives are a joke.*
*Misled by welfare, divided in the home*
*Our willpower weakened by sins derived in Rome.*
*Futures are looking grim; our children are out of control*
*Struggling to raise them, blaming the man "they say" is getting old.*
*Drugs bought overseas, distributed throughout the land*
*Drug dealers take the bait for the greed of money, while guns are put in*
*their hands.*
*Killing each other because the devils whisper in our ears*
*Racism, grief, sorrow, hatred, and despair.*
*My mind is going; it is so distraught*
*The racing thoughts make me lose my train of thought.*
*The war overseas, the wars in my hood*
*Make me realize the future is not looking good.*
*The nightmares of an Armageddon, wondering when the world may end*
*All that is going on, outward and within.*
*Everything I am, all that I've become, stem from an abusive past*
*All of those ugly traits, passed down from our former masters; memories that*
*forever last.*
*Happiness no longer, "this here" is getting old*
*I write to escape, injustices of a poetic soul.*

1

I wrote these poems during the saddest moments of my life. I was filled with grief and sorrow because I couldn't identify with what was going on, and I allowed others to break my spirit. I let so many others get inside of me and destroy my state of contempt, and it took a grand toll on me, and caused me much depression, anxiety, and confusion. These poems are from the early years and beyond, and I am going to share them with others because I know there are so many who can identify with what I have been through. Others have been mistreated and can understand where I am coming from, and hopefully, I can help others who are going through some sort of emotional, mental, or physical abuse, and they may need an outlet just as I needed it

My outlet was writing, and for those who will read this, I hope that maybe you will use it as your strength or outlet. Perhaps it may help you, or even make you brave enough to do something about your situation, but nothing that will harm another human being. What comes around goes around. You will either leave the situation, or go for help. I wish I could have, but I was not strong enough or old enough to even know how to get help. In fact, I remember being terrified, and those tears that I cried many nights because of all that was going on.

Waking up hearing my father beat on my mother, or waking up to my uncle touching me on my private parts, or waking up to a terrible beating for no reason. I was even starved by my father because he was a cruel man, and his pleasure was watching my siblings and I suffer as he brought his cruel and sick wrath upon us.

I remember being stabbed in the head with a fork, and being told not to go to sleep because he would kill us. We would take turns sleeping just so we would not die, or get stomped on with his boots that he wore in the Marines, and being thrown across a room just because he was angry.

I can remember being asked by my uncle at the age of four to have sex with him, and saying no. I remember him telling me that I had to do it anyway, and he held me on the floor and penetrated my buttocks with his penis. My father told us we couldn't go to school. We weren't allowed to eat because he wanted to teach us a lesson—based on nothing because we hadn't done anything wrong. We'd starve for many days as he ate in our faces, just to be cruel.

I can remember the drug use—the heroine, the crack, the cocaine, and the alcohol abuse that my parents had, and not having any food or good clothing because of their drug habits.

I was told by the family that we were whores and liars because they were trying to hide the molestation. I was treated unfairly by everyone in the family because they didn't like our father, and because they hated us for telling what our uncle did. To top it off, for twenty-three years, my mom called me "ugly," and I was teased about being ugly by my peers. I was victimized by my ex-husband because he decided to physically abuse me, told me I was ugly, and not worth shit. He mistreated me, cheated on me, and made me feel like I was less then nothing.

These are some of the things that I have been through, and for every cruel intention anyone had for me, for every cruel thing that I have been through, and for every harsh word that was spoken, I had a pen and a piece of paper and would write my stories, and poems. This is what I am sharing with the world so that maybe I can change someone's life for the better, and maybe I will save a life or two, or many more, hopefully.

To all those who are victims of some sort of abuse, talk to someone, or build up the courage to get the hell away! I have gone through many trials and tribulations, and I do believe the many mishaps that I have gone through have shaped and formed my personality, and made me who I am today. They say everything happens for a reason, and for many years I questioned why it had to happen to me. I later realized that it had to happen in order for me to be whom I am today. Without being abused, neglected, molested, raped, starved, and tortured, I would not be the strong woman that I am, and this poetry would not exist!

# $\mathcal{P}$ain

**June 11, 1993**

*Always saying my name in vein*
*Causing me misery; my emotions shot by pain.*
*I can't stand the way you lie in my face*
*You're afraid of the truth, but I had to put you in your place.*
*Forget you not, please. You're forgotten forever*
*I would have done anything for you, but now I could never.*
*Those raindrops falling on my window pane*
*Represent my tears of pain.*
*You used to be my sister*
*Now you're like a fever blister.*
*I hate the sight of you; I can't stand the pain.*
*I wish I could get rid of you forever*
*From my memory I erase your name.*
*It's sad it had to come to this, but forget it, I don't care*
*Just stay the hell away from me; come near my door if you dare.*
*You are no longer my sister, so please do not mention my name*
*Your mean streak got you just what you wanted,*
*So now your heart aches with pain.*

Those who have had a family member do something so hurtful such as stealing or causing chaos in their life, by doing something that devastates you or causes you grief and pain, you surely can identify with this poem. One of my siblings was very cruel to me over the years—arguing with me constantly, and stealing my things. When I was pregnant, she kicked me in the abdomen when I was twenty-two weeks along.

I had already lost a baby at twenty-two weeks that is why it hurt me so that she would do such a thing. However, several months later, I tried again to conceive and was successful. I was beaten by my ex-husband during the pregnancy, kicked in the abdomen by my sister at twenty-two weeks' pregnant, and betrayed by my other family members. I was so depressed because it felt as if I was all alone, and I found out later on in life that my sibling was jealous of me for the dumbest reason, she was angry with me because she had been trying to conceive and was unsuccessful at the time. I guess trying to kill my baby would have resolved her issue?

I had been fed up with her bullshit, and I wrote that poem about her. I was a teenage mother, because I thought by having a baby, that someone would love me and I would be able to love someone else unconditionally, and we would have each other. It was for the wrong reason, but ironically it was true, because I didn't know a damn thing about love. I was not brought up with love and affection. Today, my daughter and I are very close, and my love for her is greater than my love for life; sad to say, but true. I love life to an extreme, but I would give it up for all of my children in a heartbeat!

My sibling and I were very close at one time. We were abused together, and we went through many things in life together, but she took one road, and I took another. Her path is deadly, and her web is deceitful. Remembering a time that I purchased a car from her,

6

she sold it to me for $300.00, but when I met up with her, she told me it was $350.00 because I had to pay the man $50.00 to fix the car because he was doing work on it. She told me the price would be $175.00, but to give him $50.00 as a down payment. When I was able to come up with the rest of the money, I was to bring the car back so that the person doing work on the car could finish the work.

I got the rest of the money in a week, but when I brought the guy the money, he seemed a bit puzzled. He asked what it was for. I told him it was to finish the work on the car. He told me he had already made the repairs. I got upset and started arguing with the man because for one, he was a crack head, and for two, blood is supposed to be thicker than water. Although I knew my sister's history for lying, I hoped she had changed her ways because she was a mother now, and she had matured. Well, I guess I was wrong. When I went to go get her, she denied it and told me that he was lying.

I said, "Well, then just come with me and we can resolve the issue."

She came along, and when we confronted the man, he said, "Did you or did you not tell me that your sister was going to pay me the $50.00 that you owe me for making the repairs on the car?"

She put her head down and said, "Yes."

I was angry at that point, but to cover her ass, so that I would not beat it, she said that she would pay me back the $50.00. Do you think I ever got it back? Hell no! I was out $50.00. It wasn't the money I was angry about. It was the principle. If she needed the money to pay the man, why didn't she just ask me? Why would she lie to me? Why would she con me out of $50.00, so she could pay off her debt? It hurt me, and to this day, she is still the same way. She has done much worse to me. That was just one of the nicer things that she did. Ha! I consistently wrote poems about her mistreatment but that one was just one of the many!

My sister has stolen money from me, and stolen my daughter's jewelry. She mistreated me in front of her friends and she would constantly assault me. She knew I was afraid of her when I was younger. She dragged me once from my grandmother's house all the way to the Laundromat because I asked her to help me with the laundry. She didn't want to help and I kept nagging her about it. So she knocked me to the ground and dragged me by my hair as I kicked and screamed.

My sister and I had an agreement about a car that I sold to her while I was pregnant. She felt as if she didn't have to pay me because at some point the car had stopped working. She let some guy work on the car who didn't know what he was doing. He broke something in the car. She was angry at him but she took it out on me. She decided that she wouldn't pay me for the vehicle. I stopped talking to her and she threw a fit.

She marched up the hill to my home and jumped in my face. She began mashing my head with her hand, while my ten-month-old baby was in my arms and I was four month's pregnant.

I asked her to stop and I tried to go into my apartment to prevent it from going any further. She forced herself into my apartment, and we had a shouting match. I asked her to leave. She refused and then we began grabbing at each other because I was trying to get her out of my home. She caused a big scene in front of the children and then we engaged in a fist fight. Once again, she tried to kick me in my abdomen while I was pregnant, but I caught her foot and took her boot off. Then I beat the hell out of her with it!

I couldn't believe that she would do such a thing to me again. I didn't know why. I have tried to love her and forgive her for all the cruel things that she did to me. However, it never seems to fail; she always finds a way to hurt me. Every time that I bring up all the things she has done, she either says she doesn't remember them, or she makes up lies to justify what she has done.

She is always trying to take advantage of me because she knows that I love her and I can't say no to her. She is my sister; but I've learned from my mistakes. When she and her children were hungry, she called on me and I helped her. But when my children and I were hungry at one time, she told me that all she had was $400.00 and she wouldn't help us. She said she needed the money for her family's groceries. I begged for $5.00 because I was desperate and my children were hungry. That seemed to be too much to her, so I asked for $3.00; still she refused to help me.

Even though that happened, I didn't turn her down when she needed me for anything. To this day, I can't even get a dollar out of her.

We made a deal once that we would help each other out with our children. The deal was that every other weekend I would take all of her children and vice versa. I had her children as I had promised, but when it was time for her to take mine, she made up all sorts of excuses for not doing it. That was her way of weaseling out of a deal and it caused us to stop speaking for about a month or so.

These are some of the things that I have gone through with my sister. When I bring it to her attention, she likes to play dumb. It hurts but I love her dearly. I refuse to give up on her, but I will use caution! I continue my relationship with her because I am very forgiving and I actually cannot imagine life without her. We have gone through many trials and tribulations together. Also, I love my niece and nephews. They mean the world to me.

# Unreal

**January 3, 1995**

*So, there he goes, gone with the wind*
*Just like a leaf in the autumn air*
*As if without feelings, it seems he doesn't care.*
*All I ever wanted was you*
*The man of my dreams*
*But it seems within your heart you had a chamber of schemes.*
*Now that it's too late you want to change for your own sake*
*But I've seen your true colors, so now it all seems fake.*
*Though in my heart I feel for you*
*There will come a time you'll feel that way, too.*
*Now the only thing that seems real is your mask*
*To be a friend is all I ever asked.*
*As if you didn't know how it felt to be hurt*
*You took my feelings and pushed them away*
*As if they were dirt.*
*Now you're gone like the summer; when the winter comes in*
*You said you'd be back, but I am wondering when.*

This poem was written at a time in my life when I mistook lust for love. I was confused emotionally from the mixed signals I was receiving from the relationship. At one point, it seemed he was my soul mate, and there were continuous ups and downs. Then I married him, only to be cheated out of love because of the continuous lies, and being treated like shit. He tried to change me into the person he wanted me to be, to accommodate his lifestyle, but I left him. I realized he was only using me because he was insecure about himself. He was twenty-one and I was sixteen.

There were promises made that he would change, and that we would find our way back to one another, but he moved on! There were other poems I wrote about him due to all the heartache that he brought upon me. He inflicted continued abuse over the years, played mind games, and he also turned out to be a deadbeat father for a couple of years. For one reason or another, he decided that he was a good father—that's one of the funniest jokes I've ever heard in my life! He was in and out of our daughter's life for many years, and he used me as his scapegoat by saying that it was my entire fault. He blamed me for all of his misfortune. I think he needs to get a reality check because when you do wrong to people, it haunts you later in life.

He beat on me while I was pregnant, and mistreated me badly. Each time he put his hands on me, I was to blame. Every time he hit me, it was "my fault," but he would buy me something nice to make up for it. I was able to build up the courage to finally leave him, but he had threatened to kill himself, me, and my daughter. He put a gun to his head and stood next to our daughter's crib. He trembled with his finger on the trigger. I was horrified, angry, and scared, but thankfully my mother was there. She talked him out of it. When he put the gun down, I ran to the baby's crib, grabbed her and ran out of the room! I know it sounds cruel but I had hoped he would kill himself because I thought it would set me free. I had hatred for that man, and to this day, he is still on my shit list. My daughter carries the very same feelings for him because she can see right through him, and she is afraid of him.

I never told her anything negative about him. I always told her to respect him and to appreciate that she had a father in her life because many children don't have that privilege. She doesn't know him very well because he was in and out of her life, but what she does know about him, she doesn't like. It's the way he talks to her and the way he carries himself—as if we are beneath him. I feel nothing but sorrow for her, and in a way, I feel sorry for him. When he calls on the phone, he's always bitching about why his daughter treats him so horribly. I constantly get on her about it, but she is her own person and I can't tell her how to feel. All that he has done is biting him in the ass now. All of the grief he has caused is in my poetry. He enjoys manipulating people, and making others believe he is what he isn't. He loves to be in control of every situation. He always has to have the last word. He tries to call all of the shots. His way is always the right way, and he is very conniving.

# Why Me?

**July 3, 1995**

*I wake up in the morning feeling the world has turned its back on me.*
*Most of the time that is my reality.*
*Why me?*
*Sometimes a bird will sing by my window, and later on shit on me.*
*However, that is my reality.*
*Why me?*
*My friends and close relatives always turn their backs on me.*
*That is how I see it in my reality.*
*Why me?*
*I cannot keep a lover, somehow it seems they always use and abuse me.*
*I wish that was not my reality.*
*Why me?*
*I can't understand why my world shatters.*
*I can't understand why the ground I walk on crumbles under my feet.*
*I can't understand why everyone shows me their ass.*
*Maybe if I wasn't mentally battered I could defeat my misunderstood past.*
*Until then, I must move on and question myself.*
*Why me?*

I wrote *Why Me?* Because it seemed that I was going through a bad time in my life. It seemed as if everything was going wrong and I had no one to turn to, and nowhere to hide. I was extremely depressed and every road I took seemed to be a dead end. I'm sure many others have experienced this at some point in their lifetime. No matter how rich, poor, powerful, or prestigious someone is, they've felt the pain of depression!

I was living in an apartment with my daughter and we had no heat or hot water. We had roaches, big giant city rats, and no furniture. I was living on public assistance, and I had no family to turn to or to help me. I lived in the past and I blamed all of my problems on my abuse. I was fresh out of my marriage, and the love of my life (so I thought at the time) had married another woman who had been abusing my daughter. His wife was verbally and physically abusing my daughter, but the court system told me I had to allow him to take her to his home for his visitation rights on the weekends. I tried explaining this to the judge but I was told that I was lying. The judge didn't want to hear what I had to say. What a judicial system!

My ex-husband was such a piece of shit that he never introduced his new wife to me. I had no phone number or address for him. He took me to court for visitation rights but refused to tell me where he was taking my daughter every weekend. He was not giving me my child support like he was supposed to, and he was making my life a living hell.

I found out later that his wife was mistreating my daughter. Every time he would bring her home, she was depressed, and she isolated herself. She was two years old and talking very well. She would tell me how this woman would call her names, push her to the floor, pinch her, tell her how much she hated her, and call her ugly when her father would leave her alone with her. I got angry and wouldn't let him take her for visitations.

# Silent Tears

**June 23, 1997**

*I thought life was filled with hopes and dreams, and it was reality I wasn't*
  *facing.*
*All my life I was living in a fantasy world and it was time that I was wasting.*
*I sit back and think about all the reasons why*
*The abuse— mentally, physically, and emotionally made the inside of me cry.*
*My childhood stolen, my sanity still intact*
*The fears I had about life, struck me from the back.*
*I couldn't handle them, and so my greatest escape was to mentally run away.*
*Now I see for myself that I have to face my life everyday.*
*Sometimes I wish I wasn't born, but I live, and so life goes on.*
*Sometimes I want to take away the gift God gave, and then I rise above that*
  *and grow stronger.*
*Although life's luxuries are not in my reach*
*I take a step everyday because I know there is more to learn than to teach.*
*I know that an everyday struggle will turn out to be something good if I work*
  *hard enough.*
*God will not give me more then I can handle.*
*Sometimes I need a break because my life was rough.*

This poem is pretty explanatory. I was at a point in my life where I was confused about whether I wanted to live or die. As I explained earlier, I was abused and I just couldn't cope with the pain from all of the abuse. It seemed that every corner I turned there was more chaos just waiting for me. I was a passive person, and many people took advantage of my generosity. I had a serious problem with saying no to people because I just wanted to be liked. I didn't want anyone to hate me. I don't know why I did this. I guess I just thought I needed someone in my life. I was so lonely and misunderstood. I loved to goof off, and I masked my pain by telling jokes all the time to try to make others laugh. I was told from time to time that I should be a comedian.

Boy, do I have a lot to talk about. I used my grief and depression and turned it into jokes. I would say things like, "When my mama was a crack head, she was so far gone that she would try to sell me my own shit. One time she had a camera in her hand and told me to give her $4.00 for it. I said, "Hey Ma, that's my camera," and she said, "I know it is, but if you don't give me $4.00 for it, it won't be your camera anymore!" That was a hit with my friends.

One time my sister burned her bagel, and I made a joke about it. Everyone asked me to repeat it over and over again. There was a 7-Up commercial, and I took the joke from the commercial and made it about a bagel. I said, "Hey there, sister, what ya cooking? Yum, yum, that smells good, but mine is even better, mine is all crunchy and munchy, yo's is all gushy and mushy. Read my lips through the smoke, BAGEL. Hey there, sista, what happened to you bagel?" and then I laughed this hideous laugh that was raspy and long. I don't know why, but they loved it. I would always laugh and joke around, and so no one ever knew what was wrong. But the minute I would step foot in the house, that smile quickly became a frown. I was so sad all of the time, but regardless, I would always crack a smile in front of others, and make them all laugh!

# Changed Mind

**January 21, 1999**

*Tormented in my present, misled in my past*
*What a way to bring in the future, if the future may last.*
*No one to turn to, and nowhere to hide,*
*I keep on this mask, because of my pride.*
*Suffered from abuse, now I live in pain*
*I've decided to break the cycle; the surface is washed by the rain.*
*Learning how to survive, and think with an independent mind*
*Keeping my sanity and my thoughts combined.*
*Am I fine?*
*Perhaps, but only because I am me.*
*If your feet were in my shoes, then it is my point of view that you'll be able*
*to see.*

Well, this is another poem based on my suicidal thoughts and unwanted feelings. This one basically explains what I was saying about masking my pain with jokes. However, I said that all of the abuse, pain, and mental anguish ended with me. I decided to never ever put my children through what I had been through. The cycle of all the drug use, and abuse ended with me. I have to admit that through all of my pain, I did have an addiction to alcohol and marijuana at one point in my life. I was not quite an alcoholic but surely I was headed there. I didn't have to wake up or go to sleep to alcohol or marijuana, but I did indeed use it to take away any bad emotional feelings. One day, my three-year-old daughter said, "Mommy, I don't like it when you smoke weed and cigarettes and I hate it when you drink beer!" She was very upset and sad, and I could see the devastation in her eyes. She made me feel like I was the child and she was the adult. I was embarrassed, ashamed, and I felt very guilty. I knew that I was partially neglecting her, for my alcohol and drug abuse. That was when I knew I was wrong, and she was right. I had to stop, for her sake and mine!

To my daughter: I love you, and I am grateful for your honesty. I thank God that he sent you to me, because you are brilliant. You have courage, and you forced me to see things about myself that I was too blind to see. Thank you. You're the love of my life! I hope that anyone who reads this realizes what their children have done for them, because all of mine (I have five) have taught me something. With all of them, I have achieved something. Without them, I would not have all that I have, and I would not be "the person I turned out to become." God bless the children!

# Chapter 2:
## Hate, Frustration, and Confusion

## Bitter Kiss

**April 17, 1997**

*The truth of the matter is that our relationship started with lies.*

*You fed me dreams and portrayed false reality when you looked in my eyes.*

*There were no hope's only schemes, and immorality.*

*When I asked for the truth, you covered up the lies with things that were oh, so sweet.*

*I gave you the only heart I had and in return you gave me the bitterness of candy that was really sweet.*

*I told you the truth no matter the situation.*

*You lead me on with lies as you moved on, and expected me to yell, "Congratulations."*

*You told me you were in love with me, and that you were always thinking of me.*

*Then I caught you in your lies, and you wanted to let it be.*

*Now, I've got something that's bonding you and I.*

*When I bring it to your attention it's going to make you cry.*

*Sad because you can't enjoy it, or even be a part of it.*

*You want war; I'm finishing it because you started it.*

*I'm sorry that you're sorry; in fact, I'm sorry that your lies led to this.*

*I bet you won't deceive another because I am ending this relationship with a bitter kiss.*

Hmmm, well the only explanation behind this poem is the ex-husband! You know, he was a complete ass, and he destroyed my faith in love—well, not completely. He didn't put the icing on the cake, so to speak. Daniel, my ex-husband—I met him while taking my brother, Keith, to karate class. I had to take Keith to class every Monday, Wednesday, and Friday. I would sit on the side while my brother would participate in class, and then there he was—muscular, light skinned, handsome, and shirtless. Oh, boy, did he knock my socks off with the first glance. He would come into class confidently, and he never really smiled. He would perform his katas with ease and he was graceful and strong.

My mother always told me that I needed an older man, because a man should be older than a woman. But she never told me anything else about relationships, or any facts of life. I knew that I wanted him, and I always went after what I wanted. Whether I succeeded or not, I went after what I wanted. I told my brother, who, at the time was seven years old, to tell Daniel that I liked him. I told him to whisper this in his ear because I didn't want anyone else to hear. I was shy. I made one of the biggest mistakes of my life that day, because what looked good on the outside didn't always reflect what was on the inside, and I had to find out the hard way!

Keith, after class, runs out in the open and tells Daniel that I liked him in front of everyone. I was so embarrassed, I hauled ass out of the classroom!

I waited downstairs impatiently for my brother. I was so nervous, I was pacing. Finally, I noticed someone coming down the steps, but it wasn't my brother. It was Daniel. I was so scared, but Keith was right behind him.

He came down those stairs and he marched right up to me and said, "So is this true what your brother said?"

I responded, "Yes."

I don't know what came over me.

For one second I was brave, and I shouted, "Yeah, I like you. Do you have a girlfriend, wife, or anything, and if not, are you interested? If you are, can I have your number?"

He said he wasn't involved with anyone and we exchanged numbers. When I spoke to him on the phone, I found out that he was twenty years old. At the time, I was only sixteen. He had a birthday right around the corner, and he was turning twenty-one, but I had just turned sixteen.

We stayed on the phone all night, and we talked about everything. I thought that I was in love after about a month or so. He would take me out every weekend, and he started buying me clothes and giving me money. He never pressured me into sex. At the time, I was practicing Islam. My family and I were Muslims. I wore my head covered all the time, and I never wore revealing clothes. To him, that was exciting because he said it made me different. I do believe now that he only told me that to get me to like him because he started buying me revealing clothing after awhile. If he was sincere about his feelings toward me covering up, he would have never bought me clothing that was completely out of character for me.

After about seven months into the relationship, I thought he was the love of my life. On Thanksgiving, I lost my virginity to him. Technically, I was not a virgin because my uncle had taken my virginity, but I considered myself to be a virgin because I had never had intercourse on my own. Here is where the relationship began to get really ugly. He began to show his true colors. He became possessive and jealous. I couldn't do anything, or go anywhere without him. I lost most of my friends and I was unhappy.

About four months later, I noticed I was eating and sleeping a lot, and my stomach was getting bigger. I told him about the symptoms that I was experiencing. I was busy being a kid and an adult at the same time.

We went to Mt. Sinai Hospital in Harlem and I took a pregnancy test. I told my sister, Charlene, about what I had done, and we awaited the results. I was told to call the hospital the next day at three o'clock. The next day came and three o'clock seemed hours away because I was so nervous. At three o'clock, I went downstairs to the pay phone and my sister was looking out the window. Daniel was standing right there with me. I called and they told me my pregnancy test was positive. I stood there jumping for joy. Meanwhile, he seemed devastated, but he tried to make it seem as if he was happy.

My sister seemed happy, but at the same time she wasn't. She had been trying to conceive herself; she was wondering why I was pregnant and she wasn't. I wasn't trying to get pregnant, but it happened. I figured this was my way out of my abusive life with my mother. She treated me different from all of my other siblings. She would call me ugly, and pick on me all the time, but that is a whole other story. I was trying to figure out a way to tell my mother.

A month had passed since finding out, and I didn't know how to tell my mother, but Daniel's family had known. I was walking around the house as if nothing were different. I didn't get any prenatal care or anything. I began to feel the baby moving. I wore extra baggy clothing, and I tried to stay out of my mother's sight as much as possible.

One day on the train, my mom was on her way to work, and I was on my way to school. She had dropped the bomb on me that she found out that I was pregnant. I had no choice but to come clean. She told me I had to get an abortion, but she obviously had no idea how far I was. I decided to start getting prenatal care because my mother knew, but unfortunately, it was too late. My baby was dead inside of me. I was twenty-two weeks pregnant. I was devastated!

That is when all hell broke loose! I was never told anything about the baby. I didn't know the sex of the baby, or the cause of death. Daniel was not even with me when I delivered the child. After the birth of our baby, I noticed the abuse had gotten worse.

Three months later, I was pregnant again and I remember it as if it was yesterday—my first beat down. He and I were angry about something. He went his way, and I went mine. My sister had asked me to come with her across the street to make a phone call because we didn't have a house phone. We were with our friend, Latoya, who was trying to hail a taxi so that she could go home. I guess there were guys across the street, but we had not really noticed them because we were too busy goofing off. The next thing I knew was that I was being slapped across the face because I was apparently showing off in front of the guys.

After being slapped senseless, I realized that there were guys there, but I couldn't understand why I was being slapped because they were many feet away from where we were standing. They weren't even paying any attention to us; as well as we weren't paying them any attention. My sister just stood there as he physically abused me, and I did everything in my power to get that man off of me. He grabbed me around my neck and was slamming me into a car. He bent me backwards and slammed my head and back into the car, while he slapped me with the other hand. At the time, I was ten weeks pregnant. I begged and pleaded for him to get off of me, and that is when I grabbed his face as hard as I could with my nails, and I tried to rip his face off. I just made him slam and hit me harder. Meanwhile, my sister just stood there and watched. I kept saying, "Please get off of me. I don't want to lose the baby." Later, I found out he was trying to make me lose her.

Finally, I was able to punch him as hard as I could, and it caused him to let go. At that moment, Latoya got a taxi to stop, and I jumped in the taxi with her because I was so scared. Nevertheless, he just grabbed me and we were fighting in the taxi. Then the taxi driver kicked all of us out of his cab. I jumped out the other side, and I ran up the steps to my apartment building. I locked the door, and forgot that my sister was out there, but at that moment, I felt she was safer than I was.

During my whole pregnancy, he was cruel and mean to me. At my sixth month, we were sitting in his home, and he said to me that he was not ready for a child and that he wanted me to get an abortion. He said that he never wanted any children. I was shocked and hurt. I couldn't think of anything to do but to spit in his face. When I spit in his face, it was as if he was the dirt on the bottom of my shoe. I know it was wrong, but he had beaten me, and treated me like crap. He purposely made me angry, started fights with me, accused me of cheating, lied to me, and he called me all types of names, such as ugly, and stupid. He constantly told me I was nothing, and I was never going to be anything. For the first time, I saw that he was trying his hardest to upset me so that I would lose the baby. When that didn't work, he told me to get an abortion.

I was foolish enough to stay with him. Even at my baby shower he was flirting with other women right in my face. Two friends pulled me to the side and told me what he was doing. He told other women how beautiful they were and would lick his tongue at them. He told them that they should become models. He never complimented me about anything. He always put me down!

After I finally had my daughter, I tried to figure out a way to leave him. He was staying out late, and making up excuses. He would go to the "store" for three to four hours, and he was doing lots of "overtime" at work! We were no longer intimate, and there were a lot more arguments, and fights.

One fight was the one that put me over the edge. My daughter was five months at the time, and we had an argument over something extremely petty. The next thing I knew, I was being slapped across the room in front of the baby again! She was screaming and I couldn't take it anymore! I started packing my things, but as soon as I turned my head, I saw that he had his gun in his hand! He put it to his head. Then he ran to the baby's crib and threatened to kill me, him, and the baby, if I left him. At that moment, I was full of rage because he threatened the baby and I wanted him to shoot himself. I wanted him to die, but I didn't want him to kill the baby or me. I started screaming and begging him not to do it. I even lied and said that I wouldn't leave. By the grace of God, my mom heard the commotion. She didn't care when he was beating me. In fact, it was always my fault. However, when she heard me tell him to put the gun down, she quickly ran in the room and talked him out of it. Thank GOD!

He was crying and I was angry as hell! The minute he lowered the gun, I ran to my daughter's crib and snatched her out and told him to kill himself! I know it sounds cruel, but he put me through a lot more then I could even begin to write. Eventually, I was able to leave him, but the bad part is, not for long.

I had moved to Staten Island with my cousin Renee and her friend, Tameeka, but shortly after that, they lost their apartment, and I was forced to move in with my aunt Dawn. She told me I only had thirty days to stay, and I thought that was totally messed up because she had let so many other people stay in her home for as long as they needed to.

At the end of thirty days, I had no choice but to move back to Harlem. I went to stay at the old apartment with my sister, Charlene. She had her boyfriend staying there, along with my cousin's friend, Tameeka, and my niece. It was a three-bedroom apartment. My niece had her room, my sister and her boyfriend had their room, and my sister gave my cousin's friend a room and she made my daughter and I sleep on the floor in a rat-infested apartment. I was so angry, because I am supposed to be her sister. Although I was grateful, I was angry because when the apartment was mine, I had let her and my niece stay there, and they had their own space. We were supposed to split the bills, but I ended up paying all of the bills, and I never said anything about it.

My sister and I got into a big altercation about me and her niece sleeping on the floor, and she kicked us out without anywhere to go. I had no choice but to go stay with Daniel. I explained to him what happened and he let us stay in his apartment with him. We had decided to try to work things out, but he failed to tell me that he was already in a relationship with the woman he was cheating on me with when we were together. He called my sister and asked her what happened. She lied and said that I left. He let us stay, but I felt so uncomfortable there.

The whole time, we had sex about three times and basically he never really spoke to me or anything. He had women calling him all the time, and he told me not to answer his phone. He made me feel like a child. I wouldn't eat and I was afraid to speak. I had nowhere else to go and so I had to abide by his rules.

One day, I had an upset stomach, and I started urinating blood. He took me to the emergency room and that day I found out I was pregnant. I had a terrible urinary tract infection and I was pregnant. Oh boy, that was bad! He was furious when we found out. When we got back to the house, well, you can kind of figure out what happened. The only thing I knew was that I was being dragged by my hair throughout his apartment and my daughter was holding onto my leg while all of this was going on. She was kicking, screaming, and crying, and I was doing the same.

He reached down and grabbed my daughter, and told her to let go. She refused and called out, "Mommy, Mommy, no, stop hurting my mommy." He told her to shut the fuck up. Then he snatched her up in his arms, took her to a room all by herself, and closed the door. He came back and continued to beat on me. I tried to make a run for it, but I refused to leave my daughter. So I ran into the room where she was when I broke free from him. I grabbed her in my arms and I was trying to leave, but he stopped me in my tracks. He tried to slap me, but in the process, he slapped my daughter right out of my arms.

I looked at him with nothing but hatred and anger in my eyes. I punched the crap out of him and grabbed my daughter. We made a run for it while he was holding his face. I ran to my sister Charlene's house even though she had previously kicked me out on the street, but I had nowhere else to go. My lip was busted, and I had knots and bruises all over my body. I did forget to mention that I did bust his nose and his lip. That didn't make things any better, but I finally made him feel some of the pain he was inflicting on me, and that marked the last time he put his hands on me!

Anyway, he lied to my sister and told her that he didn't hit me, and that he had no idea why I left. However, the bruises were very apparent and I guess she felt sorry for me. She let me sleep on her floor again, not to mention three days later I had a miscarriage. I got tired of it all! Tameeka and I left and went to Albany. We stayed in a shelter. Before I left, I was dumb enough to take Daniel back. Hey, I was young and ignorant, and I thought that maybe if I went somewhere else, things would work out between us.

After living in an Albany shelter for about two months, I couldn't find an apartment and nothing was working out for me. I was broke and social services wouldn't help me at all. I called Daniel and asked him for money. He gave me $100.00, and that lasted for about two weeks. When I called him back for some more money, he told me that I was a money hungry bitch and that he didn't know why he had ever been with me. He also said I was good for nothing, and would never amount to shit. He told me to leave him alone and not to call him anymore. Mind you, I was supposed to be in Albany looking for an apartment for the three of us. Previously, he said that when I found the apartment, he would move to Albany and we would be a family again. He told me he would help me out financially. Then suddenly I am a "money hungry bitch and I was shit!" Okay, I was devastated, but I tried to make due without it. My daughter needed Pampers, and we needed food. I was out of answers and ready to give up, but I continued trying, hoping that maybe he would have a change of heart.

He hadn't called me and I was ready to go back to N.Y.C, but I had no money to return home. I felt as if I was out of luck. Surprisingly, I received a phone call but it was not a friendly phone call; nor was it from whom I had hoped for. It was my sister-in-law and she was calling me to find out how I was doing. I had no idea why she would be worried about me because I didn't think she cared.

I asked her why and she said, "Oh, I thought you knew."

I asked her what she was talking about and she began to tell me something that would cause my world to come crashing down! She told me that Daniel was engaged to be married!

Oh, my gosh! This wasn't happening to me, was it? I had no control over the situation. I don't know how but somehow I came across $50.00 and I rushed on the first thing smoking back to N.Y.C. I went to Daniel's aunt's house, and an hour later, he showed up with his fiancé's son. Boy was he excited to see me sitting in his aunt's kitchen! He was angry. He pulled me to the side and told me that I couldn't stay there and I had to leave his aunt's house. I told him that his daughter and I had nowhere to go. He said that he didn't care, and that I shouldn't have come there. I asked if his daughter could stay with him. He said no. I was stressed. I didn't know where to go, or what to do. I had no idea what the hell I was thinking about.

I was able to stay at my best friend Zima's house. I paid her mom as much as I could to stay there, but things didn't work out. So my sister and brother-in-law allowed me to stay with them for about two weeks. Miraculously, I was able to stay in my mom's old apartment as an illegal tenant. I took the apartment and I filed with the city to put the apartment in my name. The apartment was rat infested, had no heat, no hot water, and no furniture, but I had a mattress to sleep on, and I used the oven for heating the place. It was a terrible experience and it became apparent that I was unhappy. Daniel served me papers to go to court for visitation rights. I had asked him if he wanted joint custody. He said no. He only wanted visitation rights.

Three months later I received divorce papers. I hadn't signed anything and I was not served any papers. He had underhandedly filed for a divorce! I found out that they had gotten married right after, and they were living in a condominium with her children. Meanwhile, his daughter and I were living in horrible conditions. I never signed any papers nor was I served any papers, but I was divorced. According to the papers, it was because I failed to show up in court, but I never received papers to go to court for a divorce, but I did for visitation. He is a sneaky devil!

Well, I couldn't fight the divorce. It was clear to me that I had to accept what was. In the papers for child support, he was to pay $54.00 every week, but he would come over and pay what he felt like paying.

On top of that, he took our daughter out of the house and I had no phone number for him or an address. Not to mention he was married to a woman whom I didn't know anything about. I didn't know her name, what she looked like, and I knew nothing. Yet my daughter was court ordered to be in her presence because she was married to Daniel. I got to the point where I stopped letting her go, and he filed a court order for a violation of visitation. Mind you he violated also because he didn't even come to get her every weekend.

We had a well-known judge, and to me, she was a poor judge of character as well as a terrible judge. I tried to explain my situation and she threatened to have me thrown in jail. He stood on the other side of the courtroom laughing. To my surprise, the judge finally got in his behind. She told him that he was wrong for not giving me any contact information and was wrong for not paying the court-ordered child support. He was ordered to give me a number where he could be reached and the correct amount of child support every time it was given. He was upset at this and it was not surprising what he did next. He waited a week and he changed the number. Then he never came back to get his daughter.

For two years, he stayed out of her life. We didn't see him again until my daughter was three years old. For many years, he was in and out of her life. He always found a way to put me down and call me names. He would tell my daughter horrible lies, and now that she was a teenager, she doesn't want to be bothered with him. He blames it all on me, but where the hell was he all the nights when my daughter was crying for her father? I had to tell her lies to make her feel better. He missed her first graduation. He wasn't there when her tonsils were removed. He wasn't there all the times she was sick, when we were hungry, and when we were homeless. Guess what? He didn't care! That is my story about him, but there is so much more to tell. I just had to let it be known why I have had such harsh feelings toward him. I have learned to release that anger, and forgive him, but I will never forget. He is paying for his sins because the pain that he feels from his daughter's apathy is kicking him in the behind right now. I feel terrible, but at the same time, I realize that he deserves everything he gets for all of the pain and misery he caused both of us.

# Mind Deceived

**July 10, 1997**

*I've been pushed, shoved, and worked like a slave.*
*I had to fight many battles and pretend that I was brave.*
*What it all came down to was my low self-esteem.*
*I cussed and I fought to blow off the steam.*
*If I loved myself, words would not affect me just because I didn't love being me.*
*I am black, beautiful, intelligent, and special; because I was mentally blind*
*        I couldn't see.*
*I've realized there is more to beauty then what the eye can vision.*
*My inner beauty is far beyond anyone's decision.*
*Now that I'm wiser there's a lot less chaos in my life.*
*I've been through thick and thin, from mother to wife.*
*I can't stand liars, heartbreakers, and low-life thieves.*
*They go around lying, stealing, breaking hearts, and teaching the young*
*        how to deceive.*

I dedicate this poem to all of the oppressors in my life. I'd like to thank my mother, my father, and my molesting uncle. Give yourselves a round of applause.

You see, it all started from the time that I could remember, but, of course, it goes a lot further back, but I'm going by what I can remember. My mother was a beautiful woman at one time, but inner beauty should count here. In this case, it doesn't because her inner beauty was taken from her by her past. My dad used to beat her until she bled, and he tormented and tortured my mother so badly that she was deathly afraid of him. She also allowed him to abuse his children.

I remember hearing him beating her and she would scream so loud that I could feel the blows. I could feel myself trembling from fear when he was angry! Nonetheless, he would take it out on everyone around him. When my dad was not home it was a sigh of relief for everyone, and I remember this at the age of three. He was very hard on us, but I believe his drug use had a lot to do with it. I am not making excuses for him, but drug use plays a big role in personality changes.

He would write our letters and numbers on a chalk board and we would have to recite them everyday. For every letter or number we missed, we would have several lashings with a hard leather belt. That would be followed by the severe punishment of standing in the corner for hours with our cheeks puffed out on one leg. We were not allowed to have breakfast, lunch, or dinner. That was at the age of three. As we got older, the beatings were more severe, and the punishments were a lot more devastating.

My dad was put in prison for about four years, and before that he was a Marine. We were so happy when he was not home, but at the same time, we were going through other issues. It was as if we left one hell just to go to another. When my father was in prison, my mom was using drugs heavily. She would drink herself into a coma-like state. There were different men and women in the house all of the time, and we were put into a lot of uncomfortable situations. Like the one time I was using the bathroom and a man came in and injected himself with heroine right in front of me. I was about four years old at the time.

We were always forced to stay in our rooms, and often were left in the house by ourselves. If we went over to my grandmother's house, my uncle would have his way with us. He would play wrestling games with us, and it would always turn ugly because he would touch and feel us. He would force me to face the wall as if I had done something wrong.

One day, the family was over and they were all in the kitchen. My sister, cousin and I were in the room with our uncle Todd and he was "wrestling with us." My cousin didn't like the way he was "wrestling" with us and she had ran into the kitchen with everyone else. I started crying because I didn't like the way he was touching me. My uncle did his normal routine of having me face the wall, but this time it was different. He told me to sit in a chair and not to turn around until I heard him call my name. I waited anxiously for him to call me, but it seemed as if it took forever.

After awhile, I began to get tired, but bingo, he finally called my name, I thought! To my surprise, he was on top of my six-year-old sister, Charlene, and she had this desperate look on her face as if she wanted me to help her, but I was in shock! My uncle was on top of her, moving up and down, and breathing heavily with both their pants down. She was lying on her stomach, which definitely meant he penetrated her from behind. I sat there with my mouth open. I couldn't take my eyes off of them. He yelled at me and told me to turn around. I turned around so quickly he didn't even have a chance to finish his sentence.

I couldn't believe what I had seen. I wish I hadn't. I didn't know what I was seeing, but I knew it was wrong. I was threatened and told not to ever say anything or he was going to beat me. I was so scared but he had used this tactic to also get me to do it with him. Several days later, we had to go to grandmother's house and this was when he made his move.

He asked me if I wanted to do "booty," which was what he called it. Before I could answer, he told me to go lie on the bed with my pants down. I did as I was told. He came behind me and lay on top of me. At first, he put his penis in between my buttocks, and I am guessing this was supposed to make me feel comfortable. Then he told me to hump back as if I knew what that was at the age of four. Before I knew it, he was holding my mouth shut as he began to penetrate his penis into my anus. He was going pretty slowly but it hurt like hell, and I laid there muzzled and in tears. It felt like it took hours and I felt sick to my stomach. When he was done, I had semen all over me and he told me to go clean my nasty ass up. I was in the bathroom cleaning semen, sperm, and blood from in between my legs and off of my butt cheeks. I felt so disgusting and dirty.

After I had cleaned myself off, he made me come in the room and sit down. Basically he used psychology on me by saying that I would get in trouble if I told. He told me that what I was doing was called humping and that humping was something fresh, and if I told anyone that I was humping, that I would get a beating. I knew one thing for sure; I damn sure didn't want anymore beatings. I kept it a secret even from Charlene. My uncle was so devious; he talked my mother into letting him baby-sit, and he would come to my nursery school and pick me up early just to, as he would say, "Do booty!"

This went on for a long time. My mother was so into drugs she couldn't see what was going on. My mother would leave us alone in the house all night long while she was out drinking and drugging. My dad was in prison, and I had all that I could take. She would leave us outside alone and go do whatever she wanted to do. At one time, my

Uncle Steven came along and asked where our mother was. Of course, we didn't know and he just took us with him in his car to his house. We stayed there during our cousin's first birthday party.

We didn't get home until late. When we returned, my uncle told her not to beat us because it was not our fault. He told her she should have been with us outside, and of course, she waited until he left and held our mouths while she beat us. My mother was so neglectful that our abuse became apparent to her, but she continued on with her behavior.

One day my sister, Cousin Tina, and I were in the room playing and my sister insisted we look at her private area. She said that she had to show us something but we couldn't tell anyone because she would get into trouble. She said there was something wrong with her private area because she sat on the toilet at school. She didn't want to get into trouble because my mother had said never to sit on a public toilet. She pulled her pants down, opened her private area, and there it was. My sister had a substance that looked similar to oatmeal. It was all over her panties and inside of her vagina. My cousin screamed, ran out of the room, and went and told her mother.

When my aunt came into the room, she demanded to see what Tina was talking about. My aunt's eyes and mouth opened wide and she yelled and hollered until my mother came into the room to see what was going on. The only thing I can remember after that was being taken to the hospital and we were all seen and treated.

My sister had contracted gonorrhea and this is where the whole situation gets deeper. You see, my uncle was just treated for gonorrhea two weeks prior to the incident, but because my mother kept so much company, it was immediately blamed on this situation. No one even bothered to put the two situations together. They thought Charlene didn't have any idea what she was talking about, because she was so young.

Parents, I am urging you to listen to your children. If they say they were touched by someone, please jump on it as soon as possible. Children know when something does not feel right and they would know who hurt them! Not only that, they will begin to act differently around that person. As well, that person will act differently toward them. Your child will also begin to act differently. They will isolate themselves, or their personality will change for the worst (acting out, being mean, being rude, talking back, not listening, talking to themselves, being mean to the other siblings, expressing violence toward others and their toys, and other odd behaviors). My uncle started being really meant toward my sister and me in front of others. He made it seem as if we were always doing something wrong, when clearly we were not. Everyone thought we were just acting out. He was constantly making up lies about things we didn't do. He would discipline us for ridiculous reasons, and that is what he did to throw it off.

We were questioned so many times, and when my sister told them it was my uncle, no one believed her. This happened when I was four years old, and my sister Charlene was six. Do you know my mother's drugs and alcohol were so much more important than her children? The investigation never went any further, and she entrusted my uncle to watch us over and over again!

The time came for my dad to come home but we had been evicted because our home was raided and they found drugs. We went from house to house, and from shelter to shelter. It became a real headache until my mother finally found a place in Harlem. My dad came home, and they had gotten deep into Islam. Things were okay for a little while. My mother was baking cookies, bread, and cakes. We would go to the temple (mosques) every Sunday. My dad, however, was beating her from time to time, and we were being mistreated. My mother finally left him, but we were left with our father. We had to go back to grandmother's house with him. He basically left us there, and we were molested again.

My mother joined us a couple of months later and they were trying to work things out. At that time, in my father's life, he was managing a very well-known singing group and he was making a lot of money. My mother was never really home. She was pregnant with my brother, Keith, and she was doing more drinking and drugging than ever. They were never home and that left room for my uncle to have his way with us. My mother finally had my brother and we were living in my Aunt Gwendolyn's house (my mother's sister). That was the only place we ever felt safe from harm. My aunty was very good to us, but my mother was a terrible sister and mother. She would take us to people's homes and she would stay there with us for a couple of days. Then she would just leave us there with people. I don't care who it was, whether we knew them or not, we were stuck there. My aunt was the only one who would never put us out or even ask my mother for anything. I love her to death (God rest her soul).

At that point in time, I was nine years old and my sister was eleven. My mother finally moved back to Harlem and she was able to manage life without drugs for a couple of months, but that didn't last. My dad was back in the picture. He was beating on her even more, and beating on us. Sometimes we would all get beaten for no reason. I hated him so much, and would always hope he would leave so that things would be a little better.

One day after about two and a half years, my mother saved herself by sneaking out of the house in the middle of the night on Charlene's birthday. We were devastated when we had awakened to find her gone and we were left with the madman. My dad was so upset, but for the first couple of days or so he didn't torture or beat us. I guess he was trying to be nice so that he could use this to his advantage. He knew that if he could convince us that my mother was a rotten person, he could get us to speak on his behalf in family court. He could get social services to help him take care of us to support his drug habit.

Well, we fell for the bait and that was the worst thing that could possibly happen to us. After about two weeks, we were being tortured and abused. One day, my dad had just come home from work and he was angry because he had discovered that his girlfriend had sold all of his jewelry for crack. He was so upset. He told us what she had done. Well, he let her back into the house and she gave him this sob story. That was it for us. The next day he must have been having a crack fit because he just started acting really crazy. He told her that my sister and I had touched his things and if we didn't find it, he was going to kill us.

His girlfriend knew that we didn't touch his stuff, but she stood there and let us get beaten. We were searching the whole entire house looking for his jewelry that he already knew Denise had sold for drugs but he just felt like being mean as usual. We couldn't find anything and so he beat us until he saw blood. We were being punched, kicked, and stomped. He deprived us of breakfast, lunch, and dinner. Meanwhile, he fed my brother, himself, and Denise.

Denise pretended to feel bad for us but she was putting up a front to save herself. She asked us if we were hungry or thirsty, and we replied yes. She went into the kitchen and told my dad that we said we were thirsty.

He took a bucket and filled it up with ice cold water and said, "Oh, so you bitches are thirsty?"

Then he proceeded to throw the water on us. He told us to sleep in the puddle of water on the floor. Mind you, we had no heat, it was winter, and we had rats. My sister and I were terrified, hungry, and cold. Every time he would walk past us, he would torture us by threatening to kill us or by kicking us or stomping on us. He did this all night until

41

the next morning! I got it the worst because I was sleeping on the outside of us and he was targeting the person he was closest to.

For a whole year we were put through situations like this, and many others that were worse, but too painful to mention. That man played so many mind games on us. We were so afraid of him. We wouldn't even look his way when he walked by. When I was twelve years old, I weighed only sixty-six pounds because he was starving us on purpose. My mother came to our school to try to convince us to go with her, but we felt that no matter where she took us, he would find us. She was beaten by him so many times we wondered, how she would protect us? She waited so many months to come to try to rescue us, but we were in fear of our lives and we felt betrayed by her.

My father had brainwashed us into thinking that he knew our every move. He would tell us that we were not to talk to each other when he left the house because he would know. He said that he had tape recorders and cameras all over the house. He used fear and psychology on us, and we were so afraid of him that we wouldn't do anything to betray him because he had threatened to kill us time after time. My mother had left us too long, and it was too late to try to save us because our minds were under his control.

The way I feel is that as a mother she should have never left without us! I don't care how afraid she was, she should have taken us with her in the middle of the night, or at least come for us the next day with the police or something. It's clear to me now how selfish this woman truly was. We were tortured for about a year with our father, and it was probably the worst time in our lives. We were being starved purposely, beaten for no reason at all, mentally abused by being told there were tape recorders in the house, and we were afraid to speak or move without permission. We were not allowed to watch television or even go outside unless he had money for his drugs, but God works in mysterious ways.

Since my father had violated parole, the federal police came and took him away. The problem with that was that we had gone from one hell to another.

It was back to grandmother's house, and we were in our uncle's claws again. Now we were older and so there was more for him to do. He made my sister and I give him oral sex, masturbate him, and last but not least, he took our virginities.

I remember the day it happened. My grandmother and my sister had gone to Western Beef to get a few groceries. He put some cartoons on for my little brother to sit in the room and watch, and he told me to go in the room and lie down with my pants down. I told him no but he used the old psychology and said that I had done it yesterday, although I knew the day before I was forced to do the same thing. My uncle made it seem as if I had volunteered to have intercourse with him. I told him I didn't want to and he said that if I didn't, he would beat me. I did as I was told, and he asked me when I was going to let him "fuck me in the pussy." I told him no because I was scared, but he insisted that I let him. I cried and cried and he figured he would trick me into doing it by telling me that he was going to put it in my butt as usual.

He started having his way with me the usual way, and all of a sudden his penis "accidentally" slipped out and fell into my vagina. I was yelling because it hurt so badly. He held my mouth as he worked his penis into my vagina, and the next thing I knew; he was having sex with me. However, my grandmother and my sister had gotten back, and as they were unlocking the door, my uncle had jumped up and told me to go clean myself. He made me feel as if I was a dirty whore that he couldn't stand to touch. For some reason or another that was the last time he touched me. He had stolen my innocence and I was in denial about it. To me, I was still a virgin and no one could tell me any different.

My grandmother passed away after a year, and we were very sad, but at the same time, we were happy. This was our ticket out of this hell hole, and we didn't have to suffer the pain of being sexually abused anymore. Don't think that our hell ended here. We now were back with our mother!

At first, things were going okay. I had my best friends Zima and Alyssa with me to get me through the darkness. I also had their mom, who later on adopted me, islamicly as her daughter. Now they are my sisters also. Eventually my light at the end of the tunnel began to dim and my mother had started using drugs again. She was mistreating me before the drugs though. She would always take my sister's side for everything, even if Charlene was in the wrong. She would beat on me because my sister did something wrong. She would tell me how ugly I was because I looked like my father. If she had asked Charlene to do something and she said no, she would tell me to do it.

She gave my little brother anything he wanted and she would go out of her way for my sister. When it came to me, she would simply tell me no. I hated the fact that I tried so hard to please my mother but it made no difference. Then my sister ran away from home. She would fist fight my mother, argue with her, drink, come in the house high, disrespect her, bring different boys to the house to spend the night, call her all types of bitches, and so much more, but my mother treated me like crap.

I never disrespected her. I always did what she asked and more. I tried to have a mother-daughter relationship with her, but no matter what I did, she just didn't care; or she didn't approve. Nothing was ever good enough. I was in plays, and she barely showed up. I wrote stories, I wrote songs, I sang, and I danced, but no matter what I did, she never noticed my talent. She didn't care. She would brag about my sister and my brother though. She would tell her friends about how good my sister danced or she would recognize how pretty she was, but me? My mother never gave me a compliment or anything.

I felt so alone, and my writing became dark, sad, and depressing. I kept a journal, but I would always throw it away because all of the entries were painful. I would wish to have some sort of disease so that my mother would pay some attention to me. I would wonder if I died if she would come to my funeral. I would want to die just so that I wouldn't have to feel the pain of alienation any longer. When my mother started smoking crack, it seemed to get worse. It was funny how she would only steal from me and no one else. I was her target of hatred, and I knew she hated me. The only time she could tell me she loved me was under certain circumstances—I was either giving her something that was to her benefit or she was drunk out of her mind! She was so embarrassing. When she was drunk, she would fall all over the place and she was loud and violent. When she was high, she would parade around looking so pathetic.

I hated my life, and I hated her, my dad, and my uncle. I would cry all of the time. I would sit and stare out of my window and fantasize about being happy elsewhere. I would make wishes on stars hoping that someone would come and rescue me. Besides going through what I was going through at home, I had to deal with all of the stressors in school. My classmates called me a nerd said I was ugly all of the time, and they made fun of me for being different. How would I escape the hell that I was in? I don't know, but things only got worse when I thought that I was escaping.

Remember as I mentioned earlier, I thought Daniel was my knight in shining amour, but he was just a wolf in sheep's clothing. It seems I spent my whole life always trying to escape. Every time I thought I was safe or that I would finally be happy, it turned out to be even worse than the last time. I don't know why, but it seemed as if I was cursed or something. Happiness was never a word that I acknowledged.

My parents were good for one thing though; they made sure that we were educated and they taught us what we needed to know when it came to books. As far as life lessons, we had to learn that on the streets through experience. I made sure that I taught my children everything that they needed to know about drugs, sex, relationships, love, respect, compassion, and friendships. My mother spent so much time focusing on making my life a living hell.

I remember when Charlene had run away from home because she wanted to do what she wanted to do, and she was tired of my mother's bull crap. I felt like everything had fallen on me. One day I was helping my mother cook dinner and we were having a conversation. I was trying to get my point across and she didn't want to listen. I said to her in a calm and respectful way that because she never listened to us this was the very reason why Charlene had run away. She was offended and grabbed a hard plastic dust pan and smacked me in my face. I turned my head and looked at her as if I wanted to kill her. My mother was an angry woman. I didn't cry because after being punched and slapped in the face so many times I stopped crying and became as angry as her.

She jumped over the table and punched me in the face. When I fell to the floor, she proceeded to kick and stomp me. Then she jumped on top of me and punched me in the face. After she was done, I realized how much she despised me. Every time I would even mention my sister's name, it would anger her. For some reason, I believe she wished that it was me who was not there.

I always felt like my mother hated me because she would play my sister and me against each other. I just wanted to get the hell out of that house; but I was too young and had nowhere else to go. I was never the rebellious type and so I did everything that I was told. I cleaned the entire house by myself, watched my brother, took him everywhere with me, ran all of my mothers errands, did the cooking, the laundry, and held a job so that I could buy clothes for myself. I was treated badly (both at home and at school), and never had my own personal space.

One thing is for sure; I didn't do that to my children. Most of the chores I did myself, although they had their chores. I didn't put too much responsibility on my daughter because she needed to have her own life to enjoy her childhood. You should always let your children be children, but at the same time, it's very important to teach them lessons about life because they need to learn it to survive in society.

Learning about sex, drugs, and other things on the street is bad. Most of the time, you get the wrong information and also when you leave it up to your children to learn for themselves, they feel as if they are doing something wrong. It makes them very curious and they will want to try different things because they don't know about it. What better way to find out about drugs then to try it. That is why I believe that a lot of children go out and experiment with things because their parents were either too afraid to, felt they weren't ready, that they wouldn't understand, or they just didn't care enough to talk to their children about drugs, sex, sexually transmitted diseases, relationships, love, and etc. My lack of understanding contributed to me choosing the wrong type of men, and added drugs and alcohol to my knowledge about everything else on the street or by experimenting.

For the record, I never experimented with hard core drugs such as cocaine, heroine, crack, acid, and so on, but a drug is a drug! Although I only used marijuana, and I drank alcohol, it was still a bad decision and I wouldn't want my children to make the same terrible decision!

# Chapter 3:
# Bad Relationships

## Once a Fool Always a Fool, Part I

**February 13, 1997**

*You said a few words, but I was stubborn and so I pretended I didn't hear you.*
*As time went by I took your advice; I couldn't believe I dared to.*
*When all along you dragged me along and like a puppy, I followed through.*
*If I could turn back time, I wish I had never met you.*
*I guess someday you'll figure out that there's a small price to pay for treating*
        *people wrong.*
*When you do, I guess you'll be the person tagging along*

## Once a Fool Always a Fool, Part II

**May 17, 1997**

*You thought I wouldn't find out about your deceitful ways.*
*Now I feel I'm getting weaker and it has been hard for me to get through*
        *these past few days.*
*The feeling of not wanting to live anymore had come about.*
*Sometimes I wanted to yell, scream, and even cry, but I would just sit and pout.*
*I envy all the happy people because I want to feel happy just as well.*
*I ask God everyday to keep me in a positive frame of mind so my life will go swell.*
*I can't believe the anger and hatred I am feeling toward you now.*
*I feel someday I'll make you understand, somehow.*
*Maybe someday you'll look back and figure out that you were wrong.*
*Then you will figure out the fool you were all along.*

# Never Again a Fool—Once a Fool Always a Fool, Part III

**May 17, 1997**

*I thought by marrying you would make things better, but it only made things
worse.*
*Now I'm stuck with a cheater, a wife beater, and a man who steals from my purse.*
*I thought a child would hold you down.*
*It only gave you a reason to get out of town.*
*I thought by being the best wife I could be would make you mine and mine only.*
*That gave you a reason to leave me lonely, oh so lonely.*
*All these good reasons and not one damn thing bad.*
*I gave you a life worth living; you left me with a lot of little surprises and years of
sadness.*
*I dedicated my soul; you dedicated your fist.*
*I gave you my all; you left me with a bitter kiss.*
*I guess I have to live my life and hope that I will live again.*
*I gave it to you, and now I know I was a fool; it won't happen again.*

Oh, yes, a three-part poem about sour relationships. I already told you about Daniel, and you probably already know that part three was definitely about him, but there is something I never mentioned and that was about my sexuality. At one point in time I was confused about this. I figured my life was miserable because of men, and I thought I was somewhat right about this. I was wrong to think that being with a woman would be better. I noticed that many women who felt that they had their lives destroyed by a man, or that they were completely through with men, turned to women because they felt that a woman would treat them better. They were just as bad as men sometimes, and maybe even worse if you ask me.

I met a woman named N.Y.—well that is what everyone called her. She seemed like she was the answer to my prayers. She was beautiful in my eyes; she had long dread locks in her hair, was tall, thin, and had a caramel complexion, with the cutest button nose. She dressed like a man, and at first that is what I thought she was. I started to like her because I thought she was a really cute guy. By the time I found out that she was a woman, it was too late because I already liked her. I didn't care because I was curious about being a lesbian anyway.

I would leave notes on her car (actually my cousin Bertha would go downstairs in the middle of the night and leave the notes on her car's windshield); and then I would stand on my balcony the next day and watch her to see if she had gotten the note. Of course, I gave her poetry and the poems were completely anonymous because I was her "secret admirer."

Eventually I mentioned my identity and left her my telephone number. She called. I was so nervous because I had never been with a woman before. I had no idea what to say or do, and I was hoping I didn't say the wrong thing and blow it. She would call me everyday, and she made me feel really special. She told me she had a wife, and that she lived with her wife but they were not together. That was true because I would see her wife bring her new girlfriend over all of the time. N.Y and the new girlfriend would have several arguments.

She had me going for so many months and I thought I was completely in love with her. She requested keys to my house and I gave them to her. She played many mind games with me and she led me on for a long time. She would tell me she was coming over and would never show up. She would keep me a secret from everyone, and she would constantly lie to me about things. She also lied to me several times and had people thinking that I was stalking her and that I was crazy.

One day I told her I was going to visit my mother and she forbids me to go. I told her I had to and that I was staying for a week. N.Y said that if I went that I was deserting her just like her wife did. She tried to keep me from going and so she finally came to my house so we could spend time together.

We talked about having sex for a long time and I was so nervous because I didn't know how or what to do when it came to women. I let her do all of the work when it came down to it. She tied me up and spanked me, but all of a sudden her hits began to get a little serious. One minute I was being spanked and the next thing minute she was punching me in the head while I was tied up. She told me that I better not abandon her and go to see my mother. She was hitting me really hard and she said she didn't want me to desert her. She said if I left, she would beat my ass when I got back.

When she was done beating on me, she untied me and then she left. I did, however, go to see my mom and I stayed a little over a week. When I got back, she was acting really distant toward me. I figured that she was done with me, so I got a boyfriend. I messed around and got pregnant. She was highly upset about that and told me to get an abortion. Me being stupid, I got the abortion, but it was not because she had told me to. It was because the father was acting like a prick, and I refused to have another child with another asshole. I am still upset to this day about that abortion because I killed another human being who had just as much of a right to be here as I do. This was when she basically broke things off with me.

I was devastated about her ending the relationship and I realized that she was only playing me for a fool. So I wrote "Once a Fool Always a Fool, Part I" about her.

Part II, however, was about this guy I had dated for eight months and he was possessive, obsessive, jealous, emotional, and he had a problem with putting his hands on me. He constantly picked fights with me, and every time the phone rang, he accused me of either talking to another guy or cheating on him. I couldn't do anything without being accused of cheating and he was always crying because he didn't want me to leave him. Every time I tried to leave, he would cry like a baby and that made me feel guilty. So I stayed with him. His name was Terry. He was six-foot-three, light skinned, and skinny, with the prettiest long eyelashes. He also had a beautiful smile. I am a sucker for a beautiful smile.

What made me leave him was the fact that he hit me in front of my daughter. I couldn't take it anymore. After he hit me, I put my daughter in his mother's room and commenced to beat his ass. I took a screwdriver and jabbed him in the legs. When he hit the floor, I took his boots off of his feet and beat him in the face with them. I had to do this because he was much bigger then me and he definitely was trying to hurt me. I left him alone, but several weeks later I ended up taking him back.

Once again he hit me in front of my daughter and I didn't have the time to get my daughter out of the way this time. I had to defend myself right at that moment. I grabbed the house phone and hit him in the face with it. I dropped the phone and we engaged in a fist fight. I don't know how but I beat the living daylights out of him. I kicked him out of my home and told him never to call me again. He didn't listen and he would call and come to my house, but I wouldn't answer my door. When he called, I would hang up the phone on him.

I just seemed to have had the worst relationships because I had poor judgment in men. I have learned that you have to take things slow, and get to know a person before you jump into anything. If the relationship does not feel right, or if your gut feeling tells you not to deal with a person, don't pursue the relationship. Especially if they hit you, don't forgive their actions! You must leave immediately because if they hit you once, they will do it again. Then each time they will take it further and further. If they lie to you, leave it alone because they are incapable of telling the truth. One lie usually leads to nothing but a big web of deception. One lie leads to others and you have to keep lying in order to keep your lie going. To me, a liar is a cheater, and a thief.

Most men that I have gotten into relationships with either cheated on me, stole from me, put their hands on me, or used me for one thing or another. I have learned from my mistakes, and I urge any person to try to learn from their mistakes so that you will not make them again. Make sure you are honest with your children about everything because you don't want them to make the same mistakes. Its better that they learn from your mistakes. That is why you want to be truthful with your children so they will not want to make that mistake.

There were other relationships that went sour and there were two times that I was raped. It resulted in me having children as a result of it. The first relationship where I was raped was my son's father, Mike. Mike I met when I was in a rehabilitation program that I checked myself into because I was drinking excessively. I didn't want to become an alcoholic like my mother, Haleema. I was in the program for about eight months and I had accomplished more than one thing. I had gotten my G.E.D diploma, I stopped smoking, and I discontinued my drinking. Anyway, Mike and I became good friends and he was a little feminine to me. I assumed he was a homosexual. He explained that he was not a homosexual but he said that he had gone through a phase at one time in his life and he did date guys.

One night, he, I, and some of his buddies had gone to the bar to celebrate my $2,000.00 settlement that I had gotten for a car accident (not a lot of money). I had only been in the program at this point for about two months and I was not ready to give up drinking. We had all gotten a little intoxicated and we went back to Mike's house. After we got there, one thing led to another and we engaged in intercourse.

Well, soon after, it resulted in a relationship and we were happy for a little while until one day we were at the program and someone had revealed that Mike was in a relationship with someone else. I was very angry and heartbroken. I confronted him, and he exclaimed that it was true. He had no choice but to tell the truth because everyone from the program was outside and they overheard everything. He admitted to being in a relationship with Roy, and I was devastated. However, I did the right thing and I cut the relationship off. Mike had to go to a six-week in-patient program because he tested positive for marijuana and I was a little relieved. I didn't have to look at his sorry face.

I moved on with my life and I found a new boyfriend. I know now that I wasn't thinking things through. I moved entirely too fast with all of my relationships in the past. That's why they resulted in so much heartbreak. I didn't get the chance to know them.

Anyway, his name was Scott, and he had moved in with me and my daughter. At the time, my daughter was about five years old. We were happy until one night Mike showed up at my doorstep. He had finished his six-week program, but he had lost his apartment. He wanted to stay with me. I told him no, but he continued to beg me, so I told him that he could stay, but only for one night. My boyfriend, Scott, was upset with me and he slept on the couch. I told Mike that he could sleep in my daughter's room for the night, and my daughter stayed in the room with me.

Everyone had gone to bed and I just felt a negative vibe in my home. Something told me to lock my bedroom door that night. I locked the door and later on that night I heard someone trying to get in. It was Mike at the door, and he had broken the lock to my bedroom door. He came into my room without any clothes on. I told him to get out and he refused. He was asking me to have sex with him. I told him hell no because he and I were through and I had moved on. He went on and on about him wanting to have sex with me and I kept telling him no! It resulted in him holding me down and me struggling and trying to fight him without awaking my daughter. I was so afraid, and I couldn't believe I was in that situation. I tried so hard to fight him off of me but he was able to get my clothes off. Then he forced himself inside of me. I don't know why but afterwards I just got up angrily and I took a shower, went to sleep, and never mentioned it again to anyone.

Almost two months later, I found out that I was pregnant. I put the rape outside of my mind for a very long time, and I thought that my son was Scott's baby, but I had a reality check three years after he was born. The paternity test showed that Scott was not the father of my son. I was absolutely shocked and then it hit me that my son was the product of a rape. From that point on, I told my son that his father was dead.

All of that didn't matter to him because it turned out that my son is autistic and he really doesn't have a care in the world. I believe in my heart that everything that happens does happen for a reason. Scott turned out to be a deadbeat dad to his other children and many people asked me why. I don't have an answer, but Mike is in his life, and he takes care of his son, although it is clear how I feel about him. I am not sure whether I hate him or just dislike him, but I put my feelings to the side for my son. He is an okay father, but he does not win a Nobel Prize for doing his job. I still have trust issues with him. Personally, I am only doing this for my son, and maybe I am making a mistake, but it is too late to change what is done. So far he has shown a great interest in his son. I can't believe I am saying this but he also apologized for his actions against me and I have forgiven him. However, in my mind, I will never forget and that is the end of that.

# What was I thinking?

**August 6, 2003**

*What was I thinking when I opened my heart? I opened my mind.*
*I gave you my love, and I gave you my time.*
*I shared my dreams so that we could build,*
*Instead I was left without a shield.*
*Now my dreams are shattered*
*In reality my soul has been battered.*
*The only happiness I know is this hell I'm in.*
*The ruin, the pain, the hurt, turns those bright skies dim.*
*The sun is no longer shining its light on me.*
*The rain has flooded my life with grief.*
*If I had never met you I would have remained in harmony.*
*I can remember our first kiss and the first time you wrapped your arms*
        *around me.*
*A gift of love is what you offered to share.*
*Only your lies left me bare.*
*Too hurt to cry, too shocked to be depressed,*
*Through all of this, I am too numb to be stressed.*
*Now that I am out of your life, you want to hold on.*
*When you had me, you were always gone.*
*Mentally, physically, and emotionally I was drained.*
*To take you back would lead to more suffering.*
*It's time that the sun should shine bright through my window.*
*In order to be happy, I need to remain through with you.*
*What was I thinking?*

Hmmm, is all that I could say about this verse here. This is about a particular person whom I was friends with named Dick. Now, Dick was a true and endearing friend who had my back when I needed him. He and I shared some meaningful time together as friends. We slept in the same bed and never even tried to sleep with one another. We stayed up until the sun rose talking about deep life situations. He seemed like the best friend one could ever have and I enjoyed his company whenever he was around.

I was at a point in my life where I felt the need to fit in, and he was a drug dealer. I just wanted so bad to fit in. In the back of my mind, I knew that I was in over my head, but there was something inside of me that enjoyed the excitement of knowing that he was a Billy bad ass. He was the type that you wouldn't want to betray or that you would never ever cross. He was very quiet and he analyzed every situation. He was not stupid! He knew who and who not to trust, and he could read you from a mile away. He was handsome, with dread locks and his cocoa brown complexion. He always smelled fresh and he was quite generous with his money. He was a leader not a follower, but his downfall was that he was greedy.

Unfortunately, I had to move because of a tragic event. Some guys that he had crossed came looking for him at my home. They held up my cousin Bertha, my brother Keith, my friend Keisha, myself, and last but not least, my daughter. I was heartbroken when I saw them hold a gun and point it at my daughter. I realized that no one was worth more to me then her, and I had pushed her to the side to have fun. At that moment in my life, for the first time, I knew she was my light. If my light was put out, and then I would no longer want to exist. I did what any level-headed person would do. I left after we were held hostage for a couple of hours and I never looked back.

I moved much further away from where I was living at the time and I had gone back to visit after a year. I found out that Dick was incarcerated. I was hurt to hear such a thing but I had to go on with my life. While I was pregnant with my third child, I started to write my old friend Dick. I was happy to have found him and had him for a pen pal. After my son was born, it was very apparent to me that our feelings had taken a different route. I fell in love with him. We always had a thing for one another but it was never this strong (at least I thought).

I remember our first kiss by the elevator. I felt butterflies in my stomach and my heart. I had never felt this feeling before. Usually a kiss would turn me on and arouse me, but his kiss was different. From that point on, we established that we had feelings for one another. However, at the time, nothing could be done about this because we were both in a relationship with someone else. We had already gone too far by kissing one another.

Anyway, I would go on visits to see him. I would accept his collect phone calls, send him things that he needed, and I was writing to him faithfully. Most of the time he wouldn't write back, and he was always complaining because I couldn't get up there to see him as often as he would like me to. I explained to him that I didn't have the money to do what he wanted because I had children to take care of. He seemed to care somewhat but mostly he was selfish. He was not listening to what I was saying, and it seemed that he didn't really care about my situation. He would tell me to do what I had to do for the children but then he would get upset because I couldn't give him what he wanted all the time.

He started to ignore me and not write or even call me, and I would get so depressed that I couldn't eat or sleep. He would ignore me for weeks at a time until he felt like being bothered with me. He did this quite a few times, and I warned him that one day I would not take him back. I wondered how he figured he had the upper hand when he was the one in a situation. He was trying to control me from prison! I allowed him, and that is what made the situation worse. I busted my behind trying to accommodate that man and he just never appreciated anything I did for him.

We were supposedly together for three years and we came very close to getting married. His sister, mother, and grandmother liked me, but I don't think that his sister liked the fact that I had three children. I also believe that he had a problem with worrying about what others thought. Plus, he had a habit of taking his problems out on me.

One day he must have had a nasty attitude and I had just sent him a $90.00 package for his birthday. I sent him food and clothing and I only had a little bit of money left over. I decided to send him a money order for $5.00. He called me collect from prison and I thought he was calling to say thank you. Instead, he called to ask me why I had sent him a money order for $5.00. I didn't understand what he meant! I asked him and he asked why I would send him such a small amount of money. He asked what he could possibly do with $5.00. He said that I could have kept my little bit of money. I asked him if it would have been better if I had sent $20 and he said no. He said if I couldn't $50.00 or more, then don't bother to send anything at all. I was so shocked that I sat in silence for a few minutes while he went on and on.

I finally told him, "You could have at least said thank you for the package!"

He claimed that he did say thank you, but clearly he didn't. He only bitched about what I couldn't do for him and then he said it was over. Now normally I would have been devastated, but I was so tired of his crap that I said fine. The next time I heard from him was three months later. He tried to pretend like nothing ever happened. As usual, he was ignoring me, except I had moved on!

I have to say this to all of the women who are reading this—never ever get caught up with a man from prison, especially if you didn't know him before he was incarcerated. They only have one agenda and that is for someone to take care of them while they are there. They need to eat, and they need to survive in there, and using someone to get by is the only way. Nine times out of ten that is all that they are doing. Only about 1 percent of all inmates will actually care about a woman.

I have seen family members and friends get hurt by inmates. Usually it happens when they come home. After about three months, they begin to show their true colors. Most women who get involved with inmates get hurt and I am here to tell you that I should have learned from my family members' mistakes. I am pretty lucky because I was able to catch it before he got home. When he did get out of prison, he really showed his ass because he didn't even want to reconcile as friends. He told everyone that he was just using me. Well, you live and you learn. Ladies, stay away from men in prison!

Well, moving on didn't do me any good either, because I moved on too fast and jumped into another relationship right after Dick. To make a long story short, I ended up marrying him because my birth control didn't work and I ended up getting pregnant. I had not had sex for three years because of my relationship with Dick. I had been faithful and it was not even worth it. I had relied solely on birth control pills and was too stupid to use a condom. I guess it was because I was in desperate need for loving, at least that's what it felt like, but that was no excuse.

Anyway, I ended up pregnant and we decided to get married. I don't know what I was thinking but I do know I was out of my mind. I guess I was trying to get over the one who broke my heart. I loved my husband truly, but I was never in love truly. My husband had the qualities of a man that every woman would want, except in time, I found out it was all a lie.

He was dark as night with a beautiful smile. Dark brown dread locks, medium built, and pretty almond shaped eyes with long eyelashes. He was very intelligent, and I could hold a decent conversation with him. Our conversations always required deep thought and intellect. He would teach me a few things and he was younger than I was. I admired him for that and I enjoyed his company as well. It was meaningful and I felt very close to him. He made me feel comfortable when we were together and for this I was happy for the moment, until…the day we were married!

My husband called himself *Rastafari*, but his name is Jaheem. He practices the Rastafarian religion and he smokes a lot of marijuana. The day that we were married everything came crashing down and went downhill from there. He told me that he had a driver's license and he agreed to go with my father to New York City to purchase a van so that we could have a vehicle. I only had my learner's permit and entrusted him to take the $1,000.00 to purchase the $800.00 van.

The day of our wedding it was my first time meeting my mother-in-law, Grace, my sister-in-law, Jennifer, and my brother-in-law, Lawrence. After the wedding we were all headed back to my apartment and I asked Rastafari if he was sure that he was going to New York City with my father, Haleem, to purchase the van. Rastafari's mother jumped in the conversation immediately and told him that he shouldn't be driving because he didn't have a license. This puzzled me because he told me he did. His mom had just gotten back from North Carolina from living down there for three years, and when I confronted him about the situation, he responded by saying that his mother was down in North Carolina and she had no idea what she was talking about. He had gotten his license while she was living there and she didn't know this. I believed him, but my gut feeling told me that something was not right about the story.

Monday was drawing near and I needed to know what was going on. I called his mother and she explained to me that not only didn't he have a driver's license but that his permit was suspended for speeding. I asked him about that and he continued to stick by his story. He told me that his mother was lying. I told him that something was not right about his story and I asked why his mom would make a lie up like that. He tried to tell me that she didn't like me. I began to get frustrated and I begged him to tell me what was going on.

He told me that his permit did get suspended but he had paid off the fine and fixed the problem. He said that he truly had a license. I asked him why his I.D. said that it was a permit and he said because he lost his driver's license and he just didn't go down to the department of motor vehicles to get a new one. I was at the point where I was confused, so I called his mom on speaker phone. She confronted him with the truth and he couldn't deny it then.

I was so angry that he would lie about something so minor and I questioned why he would take a lie so far and risk me losing a thousand dollars. He said that he was going to tell me the truth. I asked him when he was going to be honest with me—after he lost my thousand dollars? He was supposed to leave with my father on Monday to go and buy the van, and it was Sunday! He had no answer and me being angry and pregnant didn't help the situation. My father left Sunday and he talked to Rastafari about his lie, but I was not satisfied with the talk. When Monday came along, I threw him out of my home.

That was the beginning of the end. We always argued and fought about the situation and I felt that I couldn't trust him at all. I wondered how a person could lie about something so small and not feel guilty or have any remorse for doing something so awful. His excuse was because he looked up to me and he didn't want to look bad in front of me. I told him that lying made him look horrible and I asked how he thought I would feel about the situation when I caught him in his lie. He said he didn't think about that, and I told him, excuse my expression, but I told him that he was full of shit!

All of his lies eventually began to unfold one at a time, and I was losing control. Every time it seemed I would forgive him I would find out something else that seemed to be worse than the previous situation. No matter what was wrong and how wrong he was, his mother always took his side and made me look and feel like I was the one who was wrong. She told his family that I treated him badly to cover up all of her son's faults. It was terrible! We were not even married one month and we had more problems than a ten-year marriage.

He left one day and never came back. I was so sad and angry. He left because of something he did wrong. I had finally bought a car and I had asked him not to have any drugs in the car. I also asked him to never use the car to purchase any drugs. He had taken the car to a drug spot to purchase marijuana for him and my cousin, and my intuition didn't fail me. He admitted to doing it but he treated the situation as if it was not a big deal. He said, "Oh, my bad, it will not happen again."

His lack of respect had pissed me off and when I got in his face, he punched me. I fell on the bed and then he walked out of the room.

I told my cousin what had happened and of course he lied and said that he didn't hit me. Then he became apologetic when I wouldn't forgive him. I asked for his ring, and I took mine off. I threw them in the grass because I felt that our marriage was invalid to him. I admit that it was wrong, but not enough for him to go out and cheat on me.

The day that he left and didn't come back, I found him at his hangout spot. He told me that he was not coming home to me. I was suspicious as to why he didn't want to come home. He said that we were not going to work out. I told him that we could if he would just stop all of the lying. He decided not to come home and I was extremely depressed because I missed him.

I felt that he was with another woman. A week after he left I went to his job to see if I could get him to come home. He admitted to me that he had cheated and I was enraged. I slapped him in the face and he grabbed me and choked me so hard that I couldn't breathe. I was four months pregnant at the time. He had me by my neck and my feet were off the ground. He dragged me outside and then started beating on me. The police were called and he ran off, but I was almost arrested.

I became even more depressed and I ended up in a mental hospital because I was feeling suicidal. They kept me in there for six days. He came to visit me in the hospital just to aggravate the situation even more. He made up some elaborate lie about how he had met the girl he cheated on me with at a party and they had a one night stand. I found out later that he was cheating on me with his ex-girlfriend, Bianca. He told me while he was visiting me that he didn't want to be with me anymore, and that he wanted a divorce. I cried until I couldn't cry anymore. I wished that the situation was not happening but there was nothing I could do.

When I was released from the hospital, I taught myself how to drive my car and I drove it to go on a shopping spree. Then I drove two and a half hours to Oneonta. I stayed with some relatives, and still he didn't want me back. I was in Oneonta for a week and then I finally came home. I went to Wal-Mart and on my way back, I spotted him. I was at the point where I was ready to let go of him. I started to feel much better and I was ready to begin anew. Unfortunately for me, I gave him my new telephone number and later that night he called me and asked me if he could come over. I let him come over, we talked, and then we made up.

After a couple of days with him being back home, the arguing started again because of the trust issues. I went to the courthouse to file for a divorce. I had gotten the paperwork and filled it out because I was so overwhelmed with the situation. On top of cheating, he was treating me like crap. He would talk down to me all the time, he was being very distant, he was hitting on me, and he would disrespect me every chance he got. Every time he would threaten to leave, I would run after him and beg him to come back. That became a burden.

I left the divorce papers on top of the clothing bin and forgot they were there. He came in from work and needed to go inside the clothing bin to get a change of clothes.

He spotted the paperwork and said, "What the fuck is this?"

I tried to explain why I was filing, but before I knew it he was out the door. You see, he would pick arguments and fights in order to give him a reason to leave, and this was one of those times.

He used the paperwork as an excuse to leave and I went after him as usual. I begged him not to leave and to let me explain why I had the papers. He told me to let him go because I grabbed his arm. I let his arm go and the next thing I knew, I was being choked and slammed to the ground. He sat on top of my stomach and started slapping me in the face really hard. Then he proceeded to get up and kicked me in the stomach and stomped on me. Then he choked me again and after a little more beating, he finally let me go. He walked off. I was six month's pregnant!

Everyone just stood there and watched. I was humiliated. I got up and ran in the house, but as I was running off, I noticed that my pants were wet. I was thinking that my water had broken. I was so scared. I ran back outside to tell him. Not that he cared because truthfully when I found him he told me he didn't care.

He said, "Deal with it, bitch!"

Thank God my children were at the neighbor's house because I had to go to the emergency room. I was so happy that they didn't witness what he had done.

I called my family. My mother and sister were furious. I finally convinced him to take me to the hospital. When we arrived, I lied and said that I had fallen down the steps. Just as soon as they were about to examine me to make sure everything was okay, my mother and sister arrived and they stirred up a big mess. They yelled at him for hitting me and I was trying to shut them up, but the nurses overheard. He walked out, being the coward that he was. Soon after that, my mother and sister left also. I was upset because I was left to deal with the situation on my own.

After my labs came back and the examination was over, it was determined that my water didn't break and that I had just urinated on myself. The baby was fine and I was told that if I didn't talk to the social worker, they would be forced to call child protective services. I was discharged the next day in the afternoon. I was not even in my home for a good ten minutes and Rastafari's family came banging on my door starting trouble with me.

Five of them showed up. They argued with me at the door and tried to pick a fight with me. I went outside to see what the problem was and they tried to hit me with the car. I had lied to Rastafari and told him that the baby had died and that I was not pregnant anymore. I did this so that he wouldn't feel as if he were obligated to be with me. I guess he sent his family to finish where he left off.

The next day I went outside and three of my car tires were flattened. His family had come back around and flattened my tires. I know he had something to do with it because I had never seen his family members before. How did they know that was my car? I called his mother to tell her all that had happened and she responded by saying he cheated on me because I treated him bad. His family must have heard in the streets that I treated him bad. Supposedly that is why they did what they did. I deserved to be beaten also! She defended him to the end, and I felt I was left standing alone because my family didn't do a thing to help.

That was not all that he had done to me. While I was still pregnant and about eight months along, he was continuously cheating on me. I have no idea why I would have taken him back. I had my suspicions and I got his ex-girlfriend's phone number from my sister-in-law. I called her, her name was Deidre. Deidre had admitted to sleeping with my husband and said that it had been going on for quite some time. She explained that he lied to her and told her that we were not together, but I found out later that she knew we were together, married, and that I was pregnant.

We had planned to go to his job so that we could confront him but as I was getting ready, my doorbell rang. It was her at the door. I was puzzled because how did this woman know where I resided? It seemed to me that she had been in my home before but she denied it. I didn't believe that because you don't just find a person by coincidence.

When he returned home from work, he was astonished to see us both in the living room. He tried to walk out the door but immediately I followed him and asked him why he did it. He had no answer! When he came back to the house, he took all of his rage out on me and attacked me in front of Deidre. So she was feeling that she had the upper hand because he made her feel like she was the wife and I was the bitch on the side.

We sat in my room after all of the commotion, and we asked him how long he had intended to keep up the charade. He stated, "Until I got caught!"

This angered me, and it made me feel as if I was never going to be happy in a relationship because I kept getting stuck with losers. We told him to make a choice and he chose me, but it was because I was pregnant. She left the house crying and he followed her. I sent him his walking papers because he should have never gone after her. They sat in the car for hours talking and this made me feel like shit. I packed all of his things and sat them by her car, went in the house, locked my door and cried.

A week later I was getting ready for a doctor's appointment and my doorbell rang. It was Deidre at the door and I couldn't figure out why she was there. I believe it was to throw it in my face that she had him and she claimed she was checking up on me to see how I was doing, but I never bought that for a second. She clearly didn't care about me; she was just making sure he and I were definitely through. She asked me questions about my husband and me as if it were her business. Questions like when was the last time we had sex, or when was the last time he was here, have I seen him, and has he been calling me? That bitch had the nerve to question me, but I being who I am, politely answered her the way I felt like answering which left her clueless, and sent her on her way.

I went to my appointment and I was told to go to labor and delivery because I was bleeding and I was contracting. I was only eight months along and my doctor was worried. Instead, I went home to prepare myself for going into the hospital and to call everyone to let them know it was time. I even called the creep Rastafari. He came rushing hours later and my labor pains were becoming severe. I knew it was time to go, but the minute we got everything situated, my doorbell rang, and guess who was at my door? Deidre!

I was furious. Rastafari was rubbing my back and trying to help me through the pain and she started to get jealous and came over to rub my back also. My husband pushed her off and took her outside. I don't know what was said to her, but she pulled off angrily. I cannot believe that she was actually trying to come to the hospital with us. What the hell was she thinking? My labor was horrible, and I was nervous because I was only eight months pregnant. I didn't know what to expect. I was afraid that she wouldn't be able to breathe on her own. I had never experienced anything like this before and so I had to wait it out.

Finally I was ten centimeters and I pushed out a healthy baby girl who weighed six pounds and eight ounces. My happiness was short-lived. I sent him to get some things from the house, and he took hours. I called the house and my friend Lashonda was watching the children. She told me he had left a long time ago and he was not there. He showed up hours after that and he was angry and had a disgusting attitude. He never touched me or anything and he only dealt with the baby. When I finally got home with the baby, his time there was short-lived. We got into a terrible argument and he left once again. The baby was only two weeks old and I was left all alone to take care of her all by myself. He told everyone that our daughter was not his and he refused to do anything for her. I tried to take him to court for a paternity test three times but he didn't show up for any of the appointments. I was frustrated with his sorry ass, and I decided to completely write him off.

Of course I was being dumb and I had sex with him when my daughter was a month old. I don't know why I would put myself in this situation, but a couple of weeks after our encounter, I found out that he had given me a sexually transmitted disease called trichimonas and I was mad as hell! Mad mostly at myself because I should have known better then that. I was angry because I was afraid that maybe I could have contracted H.I.V. because he was out in the streets being an asshole and not protecting himself.

After being treated, my daughter became very ill. She had a bad reaction to the antibiotics. I was breast feeding and she had gotten sick because of all the medicine that I was taking that was coming through the breast milk. She had excessive diarrhea, she was vomiting, and she wouldn't eat. The doctors really didn't do anything about it and I was doing everything I could to get rid of her diarrhea.

I ended up taking her to the emergency room because she was not really wetting any diapers and I was worried that she was going to die. I told Rastafari about it and he seemed not to care. He just stopped answering my phone calls all together. He never showed up at the hospital because he was at Deidre's house and he didn't call to check up on his daughter or anything. His mother showed up but she showed no interest in me; she was there for the baby.

She was released from the hospital after giving her an I.V. After awhile, she was okay, but I hated him. I did the dumbest thing and let him back in and took him back. I contracted trich once more and I decided not to have sex with him ever again. In fact, I decided that after I had gotten checked for all STDs that I would completely leave him alone.

One day after not having intercourse with him for quite some time, he wanted to have sex. I told him no because I was not aware of him being treated and I didn't want to contract it again. I told him that if he wanted to have sex that he would have to use a condom. He got upset, sucked his teeth, rolled over and went to sleep. He asked again a couple of days later; again, I said no, but this time he left the room. He came back several minutes later and jumped on me, held me down and forced himself on me. I didn't know what to do, but I just laid there and let him finish. I truly wanted him to leave at that point. After he forced himself on me, I had nothing but hatred in my heart for him.

Not only did I contract the dirty disgusting disease again, but he told me that he didn't get treated because he thought I was lying. I went to the emergency room and was treated for it and I threw the paperwork at him. According to the paperwork, only women get symptoms and that is why he didn't believe he had it. That is not the point. Why would I lie about something so serious? Why would you not use common sense? I'm not the liar, he is! I guess his lies were eating away at him and it got to the point where he felt I had to be lying also.

I made an appointment for us at Planned Parenthood so that we could get checked for every sexually transmitted disease. Unfortunately, we would have to wait a week for our H.I.V. test results and so I made an appointment for us to get tested at the health department. There they have a twenty minute test. He was treated for the trichomonas and then a couple of days later we went to the appointment for the H.I.V. test. I was so scared, and I am not going to lie; I almost talked myself out of going, but there was no way that I could allow myself not to know because I had four children to look after. I got up the courage to go and my cousin Bertha went also. He went in first and then we went in after him. THANK GOD WE ALL WERE NEGATIVE! I had never felt such relief in my life! Now my plan was to leave him and I went to the courthouse once again and got the paperwork to file for a divorce. I had everything planned out but then something went terribly wrong and I felt there was no end to the madness!

I went back to my Planned Parenthood appointment so that they could check to make sure I was doing okay, and to get the results of all my other tests. It turned out that I was pregnant! I was so upset when I heard this that I didn't know what to do, but I knew that killing my baby was not an option. My plans to leave him were demolished. I told him and he was ecstatic. I was not. I was depressed, and to top it off, I found out Deidre was five months pregnant. She was telling people that it was my husband's baby. I wanted to hurt this man; he had put me through so much, and now this. Once again I told him he had to go! This time I didn't think that I would turn back.

I did, however. I was taking baby steps. The minute I let him back in there was more drama. Deidre called the house at six o'clock in the morning asking to speak to him. She said she wanted to tell him about her prenatal care appointment. I wanted to choke that bitch through the phone. Man, do I hate the other woman! We argued about that and then he went to work.

She called my house again and told me all sorts of things. She said that he wanted her to have a boy because he already had a daughter. She said that he said he wanted to be with her. She said that he told her he was filing for divorce, and that they were supposed to get married. She also told me that he told her he was going to leave me soon. Being challenged by what the bitch said, I told her to call his job while I was on the way, and we would see who he would choose. She called him and he asked her what the hell she wanted. She said she wanted to know who he wanted to be with.

He told her he wanted to be with his wife.

She said, "Well, what about the baby?"

He said, "What baby?"

She said, "The one I am pregnant with."

He said, "Bitch that is not my baby. When you have the baby, call me so that I can get a paternity test. There is no reason to call me until after you have that baby!"

He hung the phone up in her ear. I sat on the other end shocked, but I knew she was lying!

She was crying to me on the phone and I felt somewhat bad for her. I was thinking how angry I was at the situation, and I thought to myself this is what happens when you sleep with someone's husband. I didn't approve of how he treated the situation. All was good when he was having sex with her, but when it came down to a responsibility; he wanted nothing to do with it. Listen ladies, if you are the other woman, this is the result of your situation. GOD DOES NOT LIKE UGLY! Never mess with a married man. They never leave their wives. No matter how many arguments we got into, he refused to leave. That made me angry because I wanted him to. I thought to myself, when I wanted him here, he didn't want to be here, but when I want him gone, he didn't want to leave. Oh, boy, what was I going to do?

I would try to find every reason to pick a fight with him so that I could tell him to get out but it didn't work until one day we got into a big argument and he hit me in the back of the head with the Bible. That was the last straw. He had to go. I was four months pregnant at the time and I was not going to be abused again while I was pregnant. He tried to work his way back in my home by leaving his clothing there when he came to see his daughter. I was afraid to tell him that he couldn't stay because I didn't want to get hit.

One day I decided to go to his job and return his clothing to him so that I didn't have to deal with the aftermath of the situation at home. He treated the situation ignorantly calling me all types of bitches and all. I got angry and I spit on the floor. I told him that is what I thought of him, and he spit in my face! I said to him that I couldn't wait to divorce his sorry ass, and I walked away. I had my oldest daughter with me. As we walked away, he followed behind us, and my daughter told me to watch out. Before I knew it, he slapped me so hard I felt my jaw pop out of place and I hit the floor.

I couldn't get up because I was dizzy. By the time I tried to get up, he punched me in my eye and I couldn't see anything. I threw a pack of napkins at him and I was yelling and cursing at him. I cursed because I was angry. He walked over again and hit me. The manager came over and asked what had happened. I told him what happened, and I left the store. That was the last straw. I called the police.

The police arrived but ironically they were on his side. I told them he hit me and my lip was bleeding. The police officer told me that my lip was bleeding because of my braces on my teeth. I was so angry. His co-workers lied for him and said that I came in there yelling, screaming and cursing, and he didn't hit me. The officers didn't do anything about the situation and the manager banned me from his job. I was furious, but the only thing that I could do was leave. Writing this is bothering me because I have to reminisce about all of these terrible events and it is killing me inside.

The next day I went to the emergency room and I told them what happened. It was determined that he had fractured my cheek bone and they said I would have to have reconstructive surgery after I had the baby. I couldn't chew, and I was in so much pain, I had to take heavy narcotic pain killers.

A week after the incident my sister and I got into it because she refused to pay me my $300.00 that she had owed me for a car that I sold to her. She was angry that I didn't want to speak to her anymore. I told her that I refused to speak to her about anything because I didn't need anymore stress after the incident, for the duration of my pregnancy. Charlene, being the devious individual that she is, walked all the way to my apartment with a scarf on her head and sweat pants on to fight.

She knew that I was pregnant and I was going on five months. She jumped in my face while I had my ten-month-old baby in my arms and put her hands on me. I gave the baby to my goddaughter and I was going to fight her, but I remembered that I was pregnant. I tried to go into the house and ignore her, but instead she forced her way through the door. I asked her to leave. She wouldn't leave. I grabbed her by the shirt and tried to escort her out but she grabbed me by the collar of my shirt and then we engaged in a fist fight. I busted her lip and she was trying to kick me in my stomach. I grabbed her foot, pulled her boot off, and

I commenced to beat her with her own shoe. Then when we were pulled apart, I beat her with the broom. She left angrily and beat up. I couldn't believe my sister would do this to me again, and I couldn't believe all that I was going through. I was so depressed I wanted to die.

Jaheem's mother and I had gotten into it also that week; it seemed that I was having such bad luck and I couldn't understand why all of this was happening. At my fifth month of pregnancy, I found out that my husband had sexual relations with my neighbor upstairs. That was on mother's day. I decided to confront her after I had the baby.

In my seventh month of pregnancy, I couldn't take it anymore. I told him to call Deidre and find out how far she was and to find out when she was due. She had given us three different due dates and it just didn't sound right to me. He said he had no reason to call the girl but I told him I needed to know. He called her, and I found out she claimed she had lost the baby two months prior to the phone call. She supposedly was due the next month. She was lying about being pregnant. He started crying and his excuse was because he was relieved, but I figured it was because of his loss. I finally had the courage to call it quits and I put him out once and for all!

I felt as if I had a heavy burden lifted when I got rid of him. I was finally free from most of my problems and his mother told me that some woman would come along and rescue him and treat him right. I let her have it. I told her that her son was not shit and that if anything I was the one who needed rescuing. How dare her! I told her off that day and it felt good. Ever since then, she had a little more respect for me, but I still have minor trust issues with her.

My family assumed I would take him back, but I never did. Even after I had the baby, I didn't. I had another beautiful baby girl at eight months and she was small—five pounds, eight ounces, and she measured seventeen and one-half inches long. I am guessing all of the stress did that. I took one look at her and fell in love. I was ashamed that throughout the whole pregnancy I didn't want her, and now she was one of the best things that had happened to me. That brings my total to five children—two boys and three girls. I have been separated from my husband for two years now and I have been practicing abstinence for the same amount of time.

I have taken this time in my life to analyze what went wrong in all of my relationships and why they went bad. I realized that I needed to do what I had to do for myself and get myself together. My relationships went bad for one, because I jumped in them too soon and never took the time to get to know them. Two, I didn't even know myself, and three, I didn't love myself enough. If you don't love yourself, you are incapable of loving someone else the right way.

Women, attract men, and if your esteem is on the floor, then you will attract nothing but trash. So women, learn to love you first! Loving yourself counts because you will realize that you deserve the best and nothing less! It took me years to figure that out. I was searching for love, but it was invalid because I lacked self-love, self-worth, and self-esteem. I am happy that I have realized this, and maybe in the future I will find someone as beautiful as myself.

# Players

**March 30, 1996**

*I'm tired of you hiding the truth and broadcasting lies.*
*You're just a thief in the night in disguise.*
*Stealing hearts and selling phony love,*
*Silently singing the words of a crying dove.*
*Painting pictures in innocent minds.*
*Molding them for different purposes because you're the selfish kind.*
*Staging acts with your little theme song,*
*Gasping for air; can't we all just get along?*

As you know, this chapter is about bad relationships, and so this poem is dedicated to all of the players in the world. Basically it says that usually men who play between different women choose an innocent victim and brainwash them into thinking that they are being sincere. They usually choose young and desperate women with low self-esteem. They tell them what they want to hear just to use them for sex, money, or a place to stay, a free meal, car payments, etc.

I am pretty sure some of you can identify with what I am saying because they have been played or someone was trying to play them one way or another. A player is quick to tell you that they have strong feelings for you and they offer you many things that they never manifest. When they get caught it is always your fault, but regardless, they just move on to the next victim.

Their victims tend to be women on Section 8, women who receive some sort of public assistance, women with children, women who have a job, women who are overweight, women who carry themselves in a demeaning manner, women who feel that they need someone in their lives, young girls who really don't know much about anything yet, and older women who are still trying to be young. I have seen all of those scenarios and I was the young sucker. They love the young girls because they can mold them to be any way they want them to be. Older women who try to be young get suckered by younger men who need someone to take care of them. Women with low self-esteem tend to get suckered into it because they feel as if they need someone to validate them and make them feel good about themselves.

Many times they will have children by many different women because they know when one door closes there is always another one opened. We women are quick to take care of a man and believe everything that they tell us because we want to feel needed and also we want to feel loved. They will play on this and run with it all the way to the bank—your bank!

Never trust a man if he calls you and the first thing he asks is when he can come over to your place. That's a sure sign that he is after one thing. Never trust a man if he tries to move in with you and he barely knows you! It's a sure sign that he needs a place to stay. Never trust a man if he can't give you his home phone number for some poor ass excuse—a sure sign he has a woman at home.

If he can't take you to his home and he is always at yours, he definitely has someone he is going home to. If you have been dating for awhile and you don't know any of his family members, honey, he is hiding you because there is someone else. If he has a habit of flirting with other women in front of you, or he cannot keep his eyes on the prize, he will be quick to sleep with another woman. If you happen to catch a sexually transmitted disease, and he tries to blame it on you, or he tells you he must have had it from a previous relationship and didn't know that he had it, he is engaging in intercourse with other women. Last, but not least, if he is always taking and never giving, baby girl, you are being played. Be careful!

# Chapter 4: Loss
## In Memory of him

**July 7, 1998**

*Here today, gone tomorrow*
*Smiling with happiness, now you left everyone with grief and sorrow.*
*The memories hurt because I know you're no longer here.*
*Thinking of what happened strikes up fear.*
*Fear of not knowing what was on your mind.*
*Fear of knowing that you were in the wrong place at the wrong time.*
*Why did this have to happen like this?*
*The tears are rolling down my face as I clinch my fist.*
*Not knowing the state of mind you were in, I don't know where you were*
     *headed.*
*Thinking of shedding my blood seem so right, but emotionally get me, I will not*
     *let it.*
*Like a tornado this hit us with a surprise.*
*Broken down by this pain there's frustration running from my eyes.*
*You left behind so many people that loved and adored you.*
*With God's blessings may you rest in peace; because that's the best thing for you.*

This brings tears to my eyes because my memory of him never fades. He was my everything and was brutally murdered. It goes to show you how uncivilized this world really is—a victim of circumstances and he was innocent. He had everything going for him. He was a chef. He was about to buy a house. He had a good job, and he was a real man.

His name was Khalil and he was my best friend's cousin—my best friend, Zima. Zima was more like a sister; her mother took me in when my mother wanted nothing to do with me. I called her mother *umi*, which means mother. I loved my *umi* because she looked out for me many times. She islamicly adopted me (adopted me in the mosque as a daughter) and took me in, along with her other eight children—Zima, Anaya, Helena, Junior, Ra'ul, Anysa, and the twins Jamaal and Jamel. They treated me as if I really was one of their family members, and my *umi* always tried to help me when I was in need.

Though I was like family, I was not a blood relative. Khalil and I had fallen in love, but we were pretty confused because we didn't know if we should or shouldn't deal with each other on that level. We knew we were not blood relatives but we also knew that we were family because I considered him my cousin also. We fought with this for years. Though I loved him wholly, I felt it could never be an "us" because of the confusing situation.

We tried having a relationship after my first marriage had gone sour but we didn't take it seriously. We both knew that it would feel weird. The relationship didn't work, and it was rocky from the beginning. We felt as if we had to hide it from everyone. I mean what people would think about me dating my cousin, although he was not biologically. Trying to explain that would have taken too much energy and so it didn't work. I used every excuse to break up with him, and one finally did work but I regretted it. I wished that I had never broken up with him. I loved that man so much. I would have to say that he definitely was my first love.

I remember when he proposed to me on my balcony. I flat out told him no because I wasn't ready. I was out in the streets enjoying the street life. I wanted to drink, smoke marijuana, and go to the club every week. I knew that getting married would get in the way of me having fun; so I turned him down. Why the heck did I do that? He was on his way to the top, but I was blinded by the street life.

Next, I had heard he moved to Florida after I had turned him down. I sometimes blamed his death on me because if I would have married him, he wouldn't have been in that predicament. He would have been home with me and we would have been happy (I hope). Unfortunately, I couldn't see that at the time. I was blinded by my own stupidity.

I always tell my children to think things through completely because you don't want any regrets. You never want to live your life having questions like, "What would have happened if I did…? Or, "I wonder if I had of done…what I would be doing? Or, "If I had done this…? Imagine constantly living your life wondering what would have happened if you had done things differently? Now wishing is not going to make anything happen, and that is rather depressing.

I would always ask how Khalil was doing because he was always on my mind. My love for him was strong but I didn't have my life together, and I wasn't thinking clear. If I had been, many of the events in my life wouldn't have taken place. However, as we all know, everything happens for a reason and it had to happen in order for me to be whom I am. Every time that I would ask about him it seemed that he had reached another milestone in his life. He was doing very well, and I was very proud of him.

I moved away from all of the chaos and I sat back and thought about the situation with Khalil. I figured it wouldn't matter if we had gotten married because not only were we not family, biologically, but I wasn't legally adopted. I loved that man so much and all I could think of was him. I called my best friend Zima to ask about him. I wanted to see how things were going with him, and I wanted to see if I still had a chance to be with him and settle down. I was told to call back in an hour because she had something to tell me. I called back after an hour but instead of hearing that he was all right, I heard that he had passed away.

I dropped the phone and cried hysterically. I was hoping it was a misunderstanding but I knew it wasn't, because it was my *umi* telling me this over the phone. I had to make sure I heard her correctly. That was one of the worst moments of my life. I couldn't swallow; I couldn't breath; and I couldn't cope. I couldn't go to the funeral. I wanted to remember him for what he was like, and I couldn't bring myself to see all of the pain that everyone was in. At that time I was suicidal and that probably would have killed me. I pretended that it didn't happen!

He was murdered by his own so-called friends and they were not convicted or anything. From my understanding, he was beaten severely with a hammer on his head and then he got up to chase the guys who had done it. They ended up shooting him multiple times. It broke my heart to hear that he was brutally attacked like that. He held on for about a week. He was in the hospital listed as a John Doe because he didn't have any identification on him. From my understanding, he was robbed. I didn't like asking about it because it was too painful to bring up for me and for my "family."

Khalil was the type of person to take care of his family. He would always check up on them and help them when they needed help. He made sure that everyone was taken care of. When he had not come by, and no one had heard from him, they knew something was up. They were looking all over for him. They tried to find out if he had been arrested or if he was in the hospital. That is how they found him. The family was devastated for this tragic loss, and though time has gone by since our loss, he will always be in my heart and in my thoughts. Khalil, I love you!

# A Poem for Tasha

**September 1998**

*For every life that's taken*
*There's a life that's given.*
*I thank my higher power that I am here still living.*
*Even though you're sad and blue*
*Thank the Lord he didn't take you.*
*I know you feel torn; your heart feels as if it were stabbed with a stake.*
*When you open your eyes from your sleep, thank the Lord that you're awake.*
*You were left with grief and sorrow;*
*The thought of being here today and gone tomorrow.*
*But remember he's in a better place*
*So take that frown off of your face.*
*As hard as it was taken, as hard as it may be,*
*Always remember you'll always have me*
*As a friend!*

The husband of my friend Tasha had been killed tragically. He was taking the garbage out and the garbage truck didn't see him. It ran over him. She was distraught and there wasn't a thing I could do to ease her pain. I tried cheering her up, but in a situation like that, there is no way to cheer someone up. I had to make her see a positive side of things to relieve some of her pain. So I wrote this poem. It made her feel a lot better and I remember that tight hug she gave me.

I have not seen her in years and I hope that all is well with her.

# Chapter 5:

## Rejuvenation and Rebirth

## What are Friends for?

**June 3, 1998**

*My best friend was Jack; his last name was Daniels.*
*I had to let him go because he used to bring me down.*
*Whatever I had I gave it to him. He was my only friend, but now*
*he lives in another town*
*When I was with Jack I used to talk a lot of smack and get myself*
*into trouble all of the time.*
*When Jack was around I'd do things I normally wouldn't do, and*
*thought it was all fine.*
*I remember one time Jack and I were at a party and I thought I was*
*having fun.*
*Once Jack took over it was all over and that's when all hell had*
*begun.*
*The next day I was sick and didn't remember what happened; I had*
*no friends to call.*
*You see, when I started hanging with Jack, I turned my back on my*
*other friends and then I lost them all.*
*One day I took a look at my life and decided that Jack was no good*
*for me.*
*I lost everything— friends, my values, and my esteem was gone.*
*I had to get rid of him but I didn't know what to do.*
*Because of my apathy for Jack, I left him alone and all of his*
*friends, too.*

*I take twelve steps every day to keep him out of my life because
friends are hard to let go.
All that he did brought me down, and that is what my new best
friend A.A. let me know!*

Did I mention that I was in an outpatient rehabilitation center? I had a choice—live or die! No ifs, ands, or buts. That was my only choice and I refused to die. I was living a life of lies, deceit, chaos, and meaninglessness. I wanted nothing but to smoke marijuana, drink, and party. I remember my famous quote, "I'm gonna die high." I don't understand why I would choose such a reckless path for myself given my past circumstances. I never wanted that kind of life for me or my children, yet I was headed down a destructive path.

My mother, Haleema, my father, Haleem, my grandmothers on both sides, my aunts and uncles on my mother's side, and some of my uncles on my dad's side were all on that destructive path. They were all on some form of drugs and they abused alcohol. It led them nowhere but dead, or homeless, and in prison. They lost themselves on the path and it caused some to lose their children; some lost their lives from the illnesses caused by their destructive past, and their sanity. I always told myself that I would never drink or use drugs. It caused so much pain in my life. My parents neglected their children and their responsibilities. It impaired their judgment, and caused them to abuse themselves, each other, and their children!

The abuse was devastating at times; sometimes it wasn't physical. It was mental and emotional. Like the time that my parents were arguing; I was making my bed on the top bunk. Our bed was by the windows which led to the basement. The yelling startled me so much that I literally let go and fell right through the window. You could hear the glass shattering as I fell through, but just in time I grabbed on tightly to the top bar of the bunk bed and I was hanging out the window. My parents heard the glass shatter and they came in the room. They were yelling at me and asked me what the hell I was doing. I told them I was making my bed and I fell back. They said, "Oh," and left me hanging there. They were bitching about the window being broken for awhile, and then they went back to arguing. I had to have the strength to pull myself up. When I finally did, I was shaking and crying because I thought I was about to die!

There was also the time my brother and I were crossing the street and a car came out of nowhere and hit me, and my brother was knocked over because I pushed him. I hit the windshield and rolled onto the pavement. At the time, I was fourteen years old and it was summer. Everyone was outside. I was so embarrassed that I got right up and limped away crying.

My brother went in the house before me and by the time I got there, the daylight was smacked out of me. Afterwards, I heard my mother asking why I let my brother get hit by a car.

I cried out, "He didn't get hit by a car. It was me."

My mom responded by saying "Oh," and she walked away.

She never asked me if I was okay or anything. I don't believe she cared at all. That was one of the reasons why I felt so alone in this world.

The tension was so thick you could cut it with a knife at times. All of those ass whippings from my dad to my mom caused me to wet my pants half the time. We were so afraid for our lives. At other times, we were so unhappy that death wouldn't have been so bad. I vowed that this wouldn't be part of my life and I lived by this. I praised God every minute of the day until...my divorce! The only thing I felt I had left was my husband, although he treated me so badly. He caused me so much pain and heartache. I felt I still needed him because I thought he loved me. Seeing my mother getting abused made me feel those actions meant a man loved you. I couldn't take the abuse anymore!

That was tragic for me, and it was no excuse. I chose that path because it was calling me. I just used my divorce and all of my pain to pick up that first drink. I could have ignored the voices, and I could have ignored that naughty little devil on my shoulder. Instead, I gave in; and with the first sip, I was hooked for sure.

When you have addiction in your family, it is pretty easy for you to become addicted, and my addiction was getting pretty heavy! I never had to wake up to a drink or go to sleep to one, but I promise you, it was leading to that. I would make excuses to drink. Every time I had an argument, a disagreement, or when I felt stressed about something, I had to go out and buy that drink.

I used to love drinking my beer, but it was the worst thing for me. When I drank beer, I would become very violent. When I drank vodka, I had the energy of a raging bull. I loved to mix drinking with smoking because it balanced the two out. Marijuana made me paranoid, but I felt like I was on top of the world. Alcohol gave me the balls to say and do whatever I wanted. That is what got me in trouble most of the time. When I mixed the two together, it mellowed out the paranoia, and made me feel relaxed. I felt like I could conquer anything, without a care in the world.

It started out with just using it to party. I could party all night long and dance the night away. I felt like I was a celebrity when I stepped foot into the club. I was at my best when I was high and drunk, or so I thought! The next day always told me that was far from the truth. The headache, the cotton mouth, the sensitivity to light, and the irritability—oh, my gosh, it was terrible. The only way to fix it was to drink and smoke some more.

I didn't think I was doing anything wrong because it was only a weekend thing at first. Then I started craving it all the time. I spent my last dollars on my addiction and clearly I saw nothing wrong with that as long as all of my bills were paid and my daughter had what she needed. Yes, my judgment was impaired and clouded. I see that now but I didn't see it then. I just wanted to fit in because I didn't have anyone. Yet at the same time, I couldn't fit in because I wasn't like everyone else. Without alcohol and drugs, I was shy.

Whenever I would drink and smoke, I felt sociable and powerful. I could be whatever I wanted to be and do whatever I wanted to do. That naïve, shy, and sheltered Muslim girl was finally a social butterfly.

It didn't become clear to me until things started to get worse. Not even marijuana or alcohol could help the situation. I would get into fights and lose because I was too drunk to defend myself (but clearly I felt mighty under the influence of alcohol). I can remember degrading myself when I was high on marijuana. I'd take my clothes off for strange men (hey, I felt as if I was the best thing that happened to them when I was high on marijuana). Things really started getting crazy when I allowed a bunch of company in my home.

They would come in and out all the time. The music was loud all the time and disturbed the neighbors. There was always some sort of chaos in my home. People were smoking in the house, and there were wild parties all the time, along with fighting. Police officers were always called, and I was on the verge of eviction about three times. I even found out that my home was going to get raided because of the drug traffic in and out. Face it, marijuana is a drug.

One day I had a rude awakening. Two guys I didn't know came knocking on my door asking me to call an ambulance. I called and I was questioned by the police. The police asked me where the person was that I was calling for and I was told that he was on my floor sitting by the elevator. I hung up the phone, and went out into the hallway to see what the hell was going on. There he was, a young man that I didn't know sitting in a puddle of blood. He had gotten shot in his buttocks. I started screaming and knocking on my neighbors' doors asking for towels. I was hysterical. Of course, I learned later on that the media had a field day with me. They said that he had gotten shot in my apartment and that was so far from the truth. Anyway, I had detectives interviewing me trying to get information that I didn't know. I didn't know what to do.

I was supposed to have a party that day but I cancelled it because I was afraid something bad might happen again. Then I picked that drink up after the police had gone, and had the party anyway! The party was okay and I had fun, but clearly I didn't learn my lesson. I should have learned when someone pulled a gun on me because they thought that I was tipping the police (someone lied to me and said this about me). I should have learned when I fought some girl and she pulled all my hair out. I should have learned when I almost lost my apartment. I should have learned when people started hating me. I should have learned when my three-year-old daughter told me she hated when I drank beer, smoked cigarettes, and smoked weed! Noooooooooooo, I learned when my daughter had a gun pointed in her face and we were about to die!

I immediately moved away. I decided that I needed to get a grip on life and get control of my life. I enrolled myself in an outpatient rehabilitation program. While I was in the program, I continued to drink, but I had discontinued the use of marijuana. I truly believe my son saved my life because it was a week before I found out that I was pregnant that I had decided to stop drinking and smoking cigarettes. I could have easily gone back but I could never hurt a child. My unborn child meant more to me than I meant to myself. I decided to give it all up for good and stay away forever.

I always said that if I had never gotten pregnant, I probably would have gone back. I had the nine months of pregnancy and I breastfeed for two years. I would never drink or smoke while I was pregnant or breastfeeding. I had time to think when I was pregnant and I realized that I was killing myself, neglecting my daughter, and disappointing her, me, and many others who might have cared for me.

I couldn't go back to that life. My skin cleared up, I started to look and feel better, and I was my old self again. I went back to God and that's where I stayed. I was on the right path, though I have had some trials and tribulations because nothing goes unpunished. I refuse to turn my back again. I refuse to ever go down that path again. I realize you only live once and you have to do the right thing all the time, even when you don't want to. Always listen to that inner voice because that voice is usually your conscience. If that voice says go left and you go right and something bad happens, it's because you didn't trust yourself or God. You have two choices in life, and I for one choose to do what's right no matter the circumstances.

I would give my last breath to save a life. I would never steal. I would never lie because it only leads to more lying and that leads to something pretty ugly. I would never judge someone because that is God's job and his job only. I would never turn someone down in their time of need unless they were trying to take advantage of me. I would never wish anything bad on anyone, and I will always thank God for all that I have because he giveth and he can taketh away. (No, I'm no saint, but I will strive to become one!)

Although sometimes it seems as if you are stuck and you can't move forward, or it seems like your luck is down, and it may seem like God has turned his back on you, keep your faith. Continually praise God, and trust in him. He knows what he does and he knows you better than you do. Your path is chosen for you before you were born and that is why everything happens for a reason. You have to go through whatever is meant for you so that you learn, live, and blossom.

God, thank you for all that you have shown me. Thank you for opening my eyes so I could see the truth. Thank you for my beautiful blessings. Thank you for the rocky times because they made me stronger. Thank you for the clarity because it made me see things clear. Thank you for your guidance so that I may do for myself and others. Thank you for the right words to say when I don't know what to say. Thank you for allowing me to be who I am. Thank you for showing me the beauty in everything, even when it appears ugly. Thank you for showing me that there is a light at the end of the tunnel, even when the tunnel seems deep, dark and endless. Thank you for allowing me a second chance to do things right because I was reborn a better person, stronger, and smarter than I ever was. I will continue down this path so that others may follow my lead to righteousness, and praise your name until the end. Thank you, God!

# Chapter 6: Realization
## I am not Just a Woman

**July, 2002**

*I am not just a woman.*
*I am a sister, a mother, an aunt, and a wife.*
*I am not just a woman.*
*I have dreams, goals, and I bear life.*
*I am not just a woman.*
*I get angry, sad, and happy, yes it's true.*
*I am not just a woman.*
*I am a person, too.*
*I am not just a woman*
*I fall, I care, I love, and everyday I rise*
*I am not just a woman.*
*You may not have noticed even if you do have eyes.*
*I am not just a woman.*
*Don't take me for granted.*
*I am not just a woman.*
*I view the world as it is round, not flat, and slanted.*
*I am not just a woman.*
*I am extraordinary just like mother earth.*
*I am not just a woman.*
*My hills and curves are here for me to give birth.*
*I am shapely, brown, and white; I come in many different shades.*
*I am not just a woman.*
*They say man was created and women were made.*
*If I am only a woman, then how did I bear man?*
*If I am only a woman,*
*How did I teach you?*
*You see, I am more than just a woman,*
*I am a queen, too!*

As you can see through some of my poetry, I have come a long way. That is why I put the dates on the verses that I have written. My style of poetry has changed as well as the kind of poetry that I write. It also has a different tone to it. Writing is what gets me through life because it is my outlet. I used to cut myself and contemplate suicide. I even prayed to God to take my life because I was filled with so much grief.

I wrote this poem because I realized that women have been viewed as inferior from the beginning of time. Men are intimidated by a strong woman and they celebrate the weak ones. Those who are weak tend to get taken advantage of more then those who are strong. I am not saying that strong women don't get taken advantage of. We just don't put up with it for too long or some don't put up with it at all. Most women that happens to appear weak and they're usually the naïve ones. However, they are naïve because either they have been sheltered or because they didn't have, or never had any good role models. Our men are leaving the homes because they are leaving it up to the government to take care of their children. They have become lazy and irresponsible.

I am here to tell you that woman are not inferior, but we are the backbone that keeps families together. Standing beside a strong man is a very strong woman. I hate that saying, "Behind every strong man, there is a strong woman." We don't stand behind anyone. There is so much racism in the world, but there is even more sexism in the world. Many men look down at women and they downplay us all of the time, but most of the time we do a better job. I am not saying that we are better; I am saying that we are equal.

Men don't realize the pain and agony of giving birth, and they don't care. They are quick to say that women are not as physically strong as they are! We are stronger! It takes a strong person to carry a baby in their womb for nine months and then to have the strength to bare that hard labor and push the baby out. Imagine carrying all of that weight for so long. The baby is between five to ten pounds, and then you have the amniotic sac which is three pounds, the placenta, which weighs about the same, and then our blood doubles in volume along with our other organs, and we are inferior? I beg to differ.

I remember a time when my husband gave our one-year-old an ice cube and she started choking. He had no idea what to do, and he panicked. I grabbed the baby and gave her the Heimlich maneuver and the ice cube flew out of her mouth across the room and she recovered. I was quick thinking and calm. He still gives me my praise until this day. I am grateful that he acknowledges that, but he doesn't acknowledge all the other hard work.

We as women are mothers, teachers, wives, tutors, chefs, mentors, psychologists, reporters, nurses and doctors in our own home. Men get jobs; and when they get off of work, it ends there. Unlike women, we have to go to work and then come home and be all of those things. We work non-stop for twenty-four hours straight. How many of you women have gotten up in the middle of the night and walked around your home to make sure the children were okay, the door was locked, the stove was off, and all was well in your home? I know I have done that almost every night. You may say that is a little neurotic, but that is what being a woman and a mother is all about.

The job requires so much, but yet we are not on the same level as men are; so they say. In all actuality, we are the ones who teach the children before they go to school. We nurse their wounds, and we nurture everyone including the poor excuse for men (most men), but we are never taken seriously, or respected. We are taken for granted all the time.

Many men don't respect their mothers, their wives, or any women. I have watched talk shows where the men control their wives and beat them. I have been there, but those men don't sit back and think about how they got here. If it wasn't for a woman, you men wouldn't exist. We could have abortions, or we didn't even have to get pregnant by taking birth control measures. If all women did that, the population would decrease and we eventually would cease to exist. So for all of you men who think that a woman is beneath you, think again!

I have let men tell me that I'm ugly, and I have let men break my spirit, but when I realized who I was, then I knew I was more than worthy. I was too good for; excuse my expression, the bullshit. I won't except less than what I deserve. If a man can't accept me for what I am, and that is a queen, then he can't sit beside me on my throne and be king.

I would rather be alone and happy, then to be in a relationship and be miserable. I can do badly all by myself! I'm not desperate; I'm beautiful, despite what I have been told. If no one can see that, then they're truly blind. I refuse to think anything less then that because my esteem has been beaten down for so many years. I accepted so much pain because I didn't think I was worthy. I thought I was too poor for a rich man, not educated enough for an intelligent man, and not pretty enough to even get a man; but now I think I'm too good to accept any man! That is one thing I have realized.

# Losing Out in Life

**August 4, 1998**

*Neglect, anger, and frustration*
*Leads to isolation and alienation.*
*Lies and deceit*
*Leads to failure and defeat.*
*To use someone and abuse someone*
*Leads you to losing someone.*
*Low self-esteem leaves you feeling depressed.*
*Not believing in a higher power left your whole life stressed.*
*Selfishness and helplessness leads you to a downfall.*
*Lack of stability and inability leaves your life in an uproar.*
*Lack of trust is dangerous because loneliness leaves the heart sore.*
*Don't you want to be free, live your life and be happy?*
*Hopes, dreams, and reality are what you need to guide you right.*
*If you choose a lonely heart, you're losing out in life.*

I wrote this poem when I was pregnant with my second child and I had come to realize many things at that point in time. I was tired of being angry, tired of not trusting anyone, tired of not being happy, and tired of being unstable. I sat back and thought about what living your life that way leads to. Believe me, I had some deep-seated issues, and I really just wanted to die at that time. No one knew how I felt because I always had a smile on my face.

After all of the drama in my life, I had to analyze some things. Believe me it was far from over but if I continued to dwell on it then I would never be able to live. I just wanted to be free from all of those repressed feelings that were buried so deep within. I didn't realize that my writing was my outlet until I wrote this poem. This poem saved my life!

I was taking a computer course at the time and we were working on a project to publish our own newspaper in the classroom. I decided that my entry should be poetry. I sat at home and decided what I would write about, and then the words just began to flow like a river out of my head and onto the paper. I couldn't stop. That was when I noticed a change in the tone of my poetry. I realized that I had finally grown up!

I do believe that without a vision you cannot move forward. Everything that has ever been invented always began with a thought or a dream, and then it became a vision. From that vision, someone had an idea and put it into words. Eventually it became a materialized thing. I have many thoughts and ideas and I could have created many inventions. However, I didn't know that many people who had the same thoughts, feelings and ideas. Some were unique and some weren't. Some people talk about it and some make it happen.

I'm a woman who enjoys writing, but I also like to be original. I know I'm very unique. I don't like to be like anyone else. I'm my own person. If there is a fight, I usually run in the opposite direction or I will try to break it up. If everyone else is wearing red, I want to wear something completely different. I always went against the grain and so I was called weird or crazy. I'm not weird or crazy. I'm me—a unique individual who separated herself from other individuals. I don't want to be like anyone else but myself.

It took me years to identify with that. I was always so depressed because I wondered why no one wanted to be bothered with me, or didn't want to be friends with me. Now I truly don't care because I've set aside all of the bullshit in my life just so that I can be my own person. I hate it when others try to be like me. I want to tell them, "Be you!" God made you who you are because that is who you are supposed to be. Every individual in this world is special. You went through hell fighting all of the other sperms trying to get to that egg. You won that voyage and it wasn't easy trying to get there, so that you could be born into this world. You may or may not make a change. For every soul there is a purpose, and many of us don't know that purpose is, but we know that we have one. So why would you want to be anyone else?

I don't want to be like Beyonce or Janet Jackson! They are who they are, and they're special in their own way, I'm special in mine, and you are special in yours. You could be the next president, or the greatest lawyer, judge, doctor, teacher, dancer, singer, etc. There is so much out there for each of us to do, but we waste our talents. We try to identify with what society expects from us. We never realize it until it's too late; the potential that we have. You are who you are. You should take your talents and go as far as you can go, and don't stop until you go beyond the stars!

Writing that poem made me realize that my degree of worth is bigger than anything I could ever imagine. I refuse to limit myself. My potential is greater than anyone would expect of me. People limit themselves to possibilities because they don't believe in themselves. Other people put them down and make them feel like shit, but you know what? Even if you feel ugly, or you may think that you are ugly, you may feel so low inside that you just wish that you would die. Regardless of what others think of you, always know that you are special and you deserve the world. You don't deserve any less than that! You deserve to be treated like royalty. You deserve respect, love, and happiness! Don't wait for it to get handed to you. Demand it and don't accept anything other than that. If you can't get it, then fight for it, and don't back down. Put your foot down!

I was treated like crap on a regular basis, and taken advantage of. I was disrespected, and taken for granted. No one ever took what I said seriously. I was called all types of names, but I sat back and realized that I deserved better. I may be ugly to some, and to some I may be beautiful, but there are six billion people on this earth. Not everyone is going to approve. For those who don't, they don't have to deal with me. For those who do, you are welcomed into my world. That is how you have to be in life because if not, it will bite you in the ass. Never look back. Love yourself first!!!

I also realized that this poem was based on all of the things that I had witnessed growing up. I have seen what lying can lead to. To tell you the truth, it only leads to more lying which ends up in disaster. I have seen what depression does to a person. I have seen what it means to be alienated by others, and then you do feel all alone in the world. I know what it feels like to isolate you because of feeling unwanted. I know what it feels like when it seems the whole entire world is causing you distress. Sometimes it feels as if the whole world is on your shoulders and you can't bear to carry it. I know what it feels like when you are feeling like the ant and everyone else around you are giants. They're intimidating and scary. I hate that feeling and I never want to go back to feeling that way again.

From time to time I still do and I try to fight it off. I'm here to tell you that being abused really does major psychological damage. It's hard to just get up everyday and live a normal life. I can't even say I know what that feels like. I can't say that I know what it is like to *not* be anxious or depressed, or to deal with stress without feeling overwhelmed.

I avoid life and people as much as possible, and I'm so afraid to live my life because I have so many phobias and fears. I just want to be normal and not be afraid to live. I want to know what happiness feels like without an empty smile. I know that I have gotten over many things, and I have forgiven a lot of people. I also have learned how to love and to forgive, but I don't know how to forget and move on. I do know my past is my past, and I have learned how to control my anger to an extent. I have learned how to love me and I know that I deserve the best of the best. I have no idea how to get it or how to be brave enough to live life to the fullest without feeling like the plane is going to crash, or I will die in a terrible car accident. Maybe I'll get kidnapped, or something will happen to one of my children.

I have realized that abuse can really damage a person's life, and I'm hoping to help someone else so that they will not have to go through life feeling so confused and being so unhappy. I know they want so much more out of life, but they're deathly afraid to go out there and get it, because of their psychological damage.

I know that going through all that I have has made me stronger, and yes, it damn sure made me smarter, braver, and a lot more cautious. It also made me insecure about a lot of things and I have in the past questioned my faith in God and my sanity! I love God more than I love anything or anyone. I know I was wrong to ever question it, but I wonder if I can ever be fixed to the point where I can live the life that I have always fantasized and dreamed about.

I'm going to live! That is certain, but I'm hoping that I don't hold back because of so many things that I fear. I'm trying to conquer that fear, and I trust my grandfather's words—fear derived from one's mind is due to the fear of dying. No one wants to die and so we hold back many things. I don't want to hold back anymore, and I'm going to do all that I've always wanted to do. Hopefully I can begin by starting a woman's movement for women like myself. We can get through all of the challenges and obstacles in our lives and conquer those fears we have, answer questions that we want answers to, and live like the queens we are—from traveling to becoming career women in the fields we only dreamed of.

I know that no matter how old you get, you can go back to school. You are never too old to learn, or to reclaim your life. You have to get out there and reclaim your life so that you'll feel good about yourself and not live with regret. Regret is a very ugly word that a lot of people live with because they wish they had done things differently. It is never too late to do things differently—just get out there and do it. Don't stop at anything. It is the only way to move forward and get on with your life without regret. Remember, actions speak louder than words. If you continue to say that you are going to change or make things better, and you don't, then those words are worthless. Words should never be worthless, or hopeless. They're priceless.

I said I was going to write a book, and I did it. I woke up one morning feeling fed up with my life and its condition. I said that I was going to make a change. I looked at all of the poetry in my folder and thought how it would be such a shame to waste all of those priceless words. I grabbed my laptop and started typing. Live your life and make your dreams happen. Don't let fear stop you! I have many fears and phobias, and I'm very afraid to live on, but I'm doing it regardless. Fear leads to failure, but to conquer it leads to success!

# Tears

Tears for sadness,
Tears for joy,
Tears for birthing a girl or boy.
Tears for anger,
Tears for a blessing,
Tears for danger, or a life's lesson.
Tears for pain,
Silent tears in the rain,
Tears for death, for life, and for gain.
Tears for getting hurt,
Tears when you hear bad news,
Tears for having the blues,
Tears for another.
Tears for a sister or brother,
Tears for beauty,
Tears for war,
Tears for love,
Tears for all of thee above.
Tears for me; and tears for you.
It feels good sometimes to cry a tear or two.

This poem is a realization of a major part of life—tears are a big release. I have cried many days and have been told that I was a cry baby; or that I was too emotional. Maybe those tears were the reason why I look much younger then I truly am. Crying relieves stress! Just let it out when it needs to be let out. Don't bottle it up!

I wrote this poem for a poetry contest and I noticed that my poetry had gotten no recognition. They wanted me to submit my poetry to them so that they could put it in their book. Get this, though; in order for me to read my own poem, I would have to buy the book and they would make money off of my work and the work of others! I had written about six other poems for their web site, but then I realized they wanted me to pay for the book that I participated in. I told myself that I would write my own book.

I would never allow someone to profit off of my blood, sweat, and tears. My poetry is from the heart, and although I'm no Langston Hughes or Maya Angelou, I do believe I have a special style all my own. I know that some of my poetry is actually good.

I would never let someone else get credit for what I have done. Isn't that what slavery was all about? African Americans worked their butts off in the fields, the crops, the land, and by building so many things, but others took the credit for it. How unfair is that?

African Americans don't give themselves much credit for anything because they're not aware of many things that we've done. That's why it's important for them to learn their own history so we can walk with our heads up—not down or slumped over as we have done for so many years. I realized that we as a people are intelligent, strong, and powerful human beings, but we've been called out of our names and we have been degraded to a point that we believe it. Men are degrading women and women are degrading themselves for men.

I have watched videos and I've noticed every year that we take more and more clothing off, and we identify with the bitches and the hoes that we are called. We don't even realize what we are doing to ourselves. When I was younger, I wanted so badly to be in the spotlight, even though I had no idea what it was about. I just wanted to be famous and I wanted to be noticed. I never imagined that I would have to degrade myself to be that way.

I used to try to get in videos when I was younger and I would try to meet different celebrities. One day when I went to a private party for a rap group from queens—during 1996—I was so fascinated with whole party scene. I had a great time especially watching them perform. I knew all the words to most of their music. After they had performed, I went to get an autograph from the main rapper. However, one of his bodyguards stopped me. Yet there were half-naked women prancing around him and all over him. Since I was dressed halfway decent, they wouldn't allow me to get an autograph.

One of his DJ's wanted to get to know me a little better and so we exchanged numbers. Then he introduced me to Mr. Sweets. I went to shake his hand and he grabbed my breast. I slapped his hand and walked off. When it was time for them to leave, the DJ asked me to come back stage to wait for their tour bus. I agreed, but I asked my cousin Tia to come along with me because I had a funny feeling about it.

When we arrived, all types of things were going on. I saw women coming out of different rooms fixing their clothing and one girl was wiping her mouth. Two girls and a rapper came from upstairs and he was zipping his pants. That's when it hit me that I shouldn't have been back there. I was about to tell homeboy that I was leaving but all of a sudden I was being attacked.

It was like something from out of a movie. On one side, guys were cheering him on, but on the other side, they were telling Mr. Sweets to get off of me. He had me by my throat and I was up in the air with my feet dangling. He slammed me into the wall and was trying to put his tongue down my throat. I was trying to scream, but I couldn't because he had his hand around my throat.

He shouted, "Bitch, this is what you wanted right, huh, bitch huh?"

I was so scared that I could feel myself shaking. If it wasn't for his DJ, I would have been one raped girl.

His DJ, who went by the name of G.M.P., shouted at him and told him to get off of me because I was his girlfriend. He dropped me like I was a bad habit and I fell to the floor. Good thing too, because I was about to urinate all over myself! That was when it hit me that all of the glamour and the money wasn't worth my integrity. To any woman who thinks that she needs to sell herself short in order to get ahead or noticed, shame on you, my sister, for thinking so low of yourself.

You don't have to take your clothes off, or shake your ass to get noticed. If that is what these men are making us do, then maybe we should take a stand and fight for our respect. Most women wouldn't want to do that because they're afraid of losing something. If you're degrading yourself to keep a man, or to please a man, then he is not worth your time or energy. I will continue to state this to anyone—including men. Please learn to love you because that is the key ingredient to living.

Without self-love, you have self-hatred, and that can cause many problems for you and others. For instance, if you don't believe in yourself, then you're liable to either sell yourself short or pick up a bad habit just to have confidence. Alcohol is a fine example. When I used to drink, it gave me courage, and then later on, a bad headache.

Marijuana made me feel like I could do anything, but now I have serious memory issues.

If I had loved myself sooner, then maybe I wouldn't have had the problems that I had. Everything happens for a reason and I wouldn't be writing this book. My goal is to help others. If I can't help millions, I hope that God allows me to help at least one person. Then maybe they could use this knowledge to help many others who need it.

# Is There More?

*I need to come to terms that this is my reality.*
*I try to live a virtuous life and leave behind the immorality.*
*I'm hoping there is much more to this*
*Cooking, cleaning, and ironing the clothes until they're nice and crisp.*
*Helping with homework, dressing the kids*
*Making ends meet and putting food in the fridge;*
*I didn't ask for this; my frustration is my pain.*
*I wanted the whole package, but I only have myself to blame.*
*I allowed too much, and settled for much less.*
*I wish I knew then what I know now because I would only choose what's*
       *best.*
*I wanted the husband, the house, the dog, and the car.*
*Instead I have not all that I wanted, by far.*
*I love my children but half of our family is gone.*
*Daddy dearest left us hanging and now I have to stay strong.*
*I'm more than just a mother; I'm a father, too.*
*I hold this family together with love; I don't need glue.*
*I pull together resources; I struggle to keep their bellies full.*
*I make sure the rent is paid and all other bills when they're due.*
*I kiss boo boo's, wipe tears, and deal with certain fears.*
*I go to school meetings, recitals, and plays so they know someone cares.*
*I sew many holes, dictate, and mentor all their needs.*
*I'm not a superwoman, and I don't need an award for my deeds.*
*I'm just doing what needs to be done without any doubt.*
*I don't run away from my responsibilities; that is the coward's way out.*
*I enjoy what I do, though it may be stressful at times.*
*I escape mentally by fantasizing about life sometimes.*
*I fantasize about being rich, falling in love, and happiness.*

*Only I'm poor, bitter, and dealing alone with all of this.*
*I'm grateful for all that I have and all that I have been through.*
*It made me realize my potential and I'm going to get everything that I*
        *want; if it's the last thing that I do.*
*Before I leave this earth and take that last breath,*
*I will accomplish all of my goals before I rest.*
*I'm who I am and I will fulfill my destiny.*
*My life is not meaningless; my essence will be my epiphany!*

I have realized that I'm someone. I'm important, and my life has purpose. Everyone on this planet has a purpose. We are all here for one reason or another. We are all special! Our lives are not meaningless; we are who we are with and without imperfections. God made it so that we are here and now we all have to fulfill our destinies.

It was told to me that at the age of thirty we begin to have an epiphany, and it was at that age that I realized I wanted to try to reach other human beings somehow and change things for the better. I have always tried to do that, but for some reason all of my attempts failed and I had many distractions. Now, I'm hoping to make others realize that they're special and that they don't have to put up with other people's crap.

You're entitled to live a decent life and be happy. You are entitled to freedom, respect, and love. Stand up for yourself. Be assertive, not aggressive and fight respectfully for what you want out of life. Not all humans have to struggle to get what they want out of life. Some are born with a silver spoon in their mouths, but for those of us who were born into poverty; we have to have our minds set on making a difference in order to do so. You don't have to become a product of your environment. You can finish school, go to college, and make a wonderful career for yourself. You may even want to become an entertainer! Whatever your goal is, you must dream before it becomes a reality. So follow your dreams and don't give up. It's never too late to make your dreams come true.

I have seen sixty-year-olds in college and it didn't seem to bother them. Therefore, it shouldn't bother you! I'm getting a late start because I wasn't doing what I was supposed to. I was too busy trying to fit in, and living in my past. I made excuses. I was also fighting with depression because of my past, and my addictions.

Although these things came into play, I didn't give up. I will continue to try to become successful in all of my endeavors. I'm hoping that my children make good choices and do the right thing. I'm teaching them as much as I can. You can bring a horse to the water, but you cannot make him drink it. In other words, I can teach them all of the right things to do and lead them down all of the right roads, but I cannot make them do the right things.

I decided to do what is right because looking at my parents' past, I have realized that they're the way they are because of the things that happened to them, and the way that they were brought up. There was physical, mental, and drug abuse. It was a cycle, but the cycle ends here! In order for my children to grow up right, I will have to live right and that is the very reason that I am living right. I need to become a positive role model for my children's sake, and for mine!

Every choice that we make has consequences. Once we act out on them, whether positive or negative, we need to think before we do. We don't want any negative consequences. If you want your children to make positive choices in their lives, then you have to make positive choices in yours. Remember, our children look up to us and they learn everything they do from us! You can't tell your children not to drink, or do drugs while you're holding a bottle of liquor in your hand and stabbing a needle into your arm. Children are not stupid, and they don't learn from our mistakes. They tend to make the same mistakes. So we have to become a positive influence in our children's lives if we want them to make the right choices in life!

# Chapter 7: My Saviors

## My Saviors

**October 19, 2007**

*You are my first love; you opened my eyes to a whole new world.*
*You made me into a woman when I was just a girl.*
*You showed me pure love because I didn't have a clue.*
*You were a gift more precious then diamonds, a priceless gift that's true.*
*Your smile alone made me see clear through the fog.*
*You gave me strength when I was weak and life when I felt like a bump on a log.*
*You are my light when there is darkness all around.*
*You bring me such joy even when it seems the world brings me down.*
*You gave me the will to live when all else failed.*
*You showed me what kindness is even when all others bailed.*
*You made me want to conquer all of my fears; so that I could be all that I could,*
        *because of my love for you.*
*You showed me that I could do anything; our bond holds us tighter then glue.*
*Because of you, I love myself.*
*You made me want more out of life, and you helped me to see I needed no one else.*
*You saw my love; it was us against this hard, cold world.*
*I have five reasons to get through it all— two boys, and three girls.*
*I value your strengths; because of it, you all gave me so much more.*
*You made me understand my degree of worth, all five of you I adore.*
*Your hugs and kisses make me feel complete.*
*I love every bit of you, from your beautiful eyes down to your cute little feet.*
*If it wasn't for you; we wouldn't have all that we do.*
*You made me want to do the right thing so that I can be a better woman for you.*
*My first child made me a woman.*
*My second opened my eyes.*
*My third made me push forward.*

121

*My fourth made me wise.*
*And last but not least my baby brought me so much joy.*
*Oh, my children, you are so precious, my three girls and two boys.*
*Five is my lucky number; number five brings music to my ears.*
*You all hold the key to my heart dividing my love between you; but wholeheartedly*
   *I love you all so dear.*
*I feel you are all God's gift to me; he did me a wonderful favor.*
*God, I want to thank you for my five beautiful saviors!*

It is not hard to tell why I wrote this poem. I wrote this poem about the loves of my life—my children! I just woke up one morning and scratched it right out of my head. God is my witness that my children mean the world to me. I never thought that I could ever summarize and put how I feel into words. I always thought the way I felt about my children was indescribable; but it is not. I had to find a way to put it together.

My inspiration was a bird. I was looking out the window that morning and it was just so beautiful. I saw a bird that was watching me as I was watching it. That's when the words came to me.

It wasn't hard because I love them more then I love myself, and I love myself very much.

My first child is my daughter. She is a teenager and we call her EE. She is the reason I became a woman. I was so immature before her. When she was born, I was drugged and I don't remember much, but I do remember that pain! Thirteen hours of pure hell, and then I became very ill. They kept her from me for two days. I didn't even remember what she looked like, but I was too sick to do anything about it. When they brought her to me, I thought that she was the Spanish woman's baby in the bed across from me. But when they put her in my arms, I took one look at her and knew she was mine.

I fell in love instantly, and from that moment, I never put her down. I was so attached to her that I asked God to never let her feel pain. I wanted to feel all of her pain and get all of her ailments so that she would never suffer. This little angel that I was holding I thought should never have to suffer. I will suffer for her!

She made me realize that it was time to grow up, and so I became a woman at that very moment when I looked in her eyes. Children change you whether you want them to or not, but she made me want so much more for her. That is why I left my ex-husband, because he was hurting her by hurting me. I felt her pain, and I witnessed the terror in her face. Those alone made me want to leave. At that moment while he was beating me, I had a flashback of when my parents were fighting. I remembered how terrified I was. It was then I realized that no child should suffer like that. I promised I would never allow her to hurt that way again.

Of course, I played myself when I started being foolish. I hurt her in the worst way possible by neglecting her just so that I could party, get high, and drink. I would leave her with my aunt all the time and I never spent much time with her. Thank God I didn't damage her too much because I realized what I was doing before it was too late! I'm ashamed that I would even do it for the time period that I did. I was never supposed to hurt my child!

With her I see the side of me that was beaten out of me. She is outspoken, and she never lets people take advantage of her or even me. My daughter will speak up for me because she feels she needs to protect me from people who are always taking advantage of me. I have a way of saying things to people and they never take me seriously. However, they will not play with my daughter like that. She is strong, brave, and very beautiful!

My second child is special to me even though he is a product of rape. I love him so much! He is eight years old and he is very bright. He is also autistic and he lives in his own world entirely, but he is a genius! I hate when he is made fun of or when people treat him differently. He has a lovely personality. He is very generous, but he cannot stand to be around too many people at a time, and he loves his own space.

I don't treat him any differently from the others just because he is autistic. I don't allow others to treat him any differently, either, although my son has suffered from discrimination. One day at school, a little boy and my son were fighting over a jacket. My son was certain it was his jacket, but the little boy insisted that it was his. Instead of the teacher taking the jacket and holding onto it until one of the parents came to claim it, she took it upon herself to give it to the other little boy. Just because my son has autism doesn't make him stupid!

My son was so upset after school. When he explained it to me, I had to pretend I wasn't upset, and I confronted the teacher. She commented that she gave it to the little boy because he said it was his, but my son also said it was his. Okay, I guess my son doesn't know anything because of his disorder, but autism doesn't mean that you can't comprehend; it means that you view the world differently and he has sensory issues. He cannot stand certain noises; he doesn't like to be too social, and he can't stand certain clothes. He doesn't understand the context of a joke and he takes everything literally. If you ask him why the chicken crossed the road, he will ask you where the chicken is.

Anyway, the teacher said that she had to get the jacket from the little boy the next day because he had gone home already. As we were leaving, she noticed the little boy had not gone home and she was able to retrieve the jacket. I took one look at the jacket and recognized that it was my son's jacket. I confiscated the jacket and the teacher said that she thought it was the little boy's jacket because he had a jacket just like his.

I went home and wrote the teacher a nice letter and gave it to her the next day at school. I noticed the little boy was wearing his jacket, and I flipped. I was so upset because the jacket looked nothing like my son's jacket. My son's jacket was a pullover jacket that was dark blue and burgundy; the little boy's jacket was neon orange and royal blue and had a full zipper in the front. That is when I knew that the teacher didn't believe my son because she is ignorant, and prejudiced!

I realized at that moment that I had to protect him from people like her. He had to be removed from that class because the teacher would always believe others over him, just the way that the police officers did when he was abused. My son was abused, but because he is autistic, the police said that they couldn't use his testimony because of his autism. The person who did it was later convicted because they had done it to someone else.

My son didn't get justice because he was autistic. What the hell is wrong with people? I will protect him until the day I die because I owe him that. He saved my life! When I was out and about, and being foolish, I wanted to stop but I just couldn't. I needed a reason but I knew that I would continue drinking, smoking marijuana, and getting into trouble.

I prayed to God all the time and asked him to help me so that I could help myself to discontinue drinking, getting high and being stupid. I made the choice to stop, but what would prevent me from going back to my old ways? A week after I decided to stop being foolish, I found out that I was pregnant. If I had not been, I would have easily fallen back into the stereotypical bracket—a single mom doing nothing with her life but messing it up, on welfare, and a drug user. Whether I like it or not, marijuana and alcohol are drugs! A drug is anything that you can get addicted to, including pharmaceuticals.

After I found out that I was pregnant, I knew that having a life inside of me was a very beautiful thing. I couldn't endanger my child's life. I never went back to that lifestyle again. I thank

God for giving him to me because I changed myself for the better because of him.

Jah-jah changed my life and I see the intellectual side of me in him. He can figure out a video game within five minutes and beat the game within three hours. He is my genius, and I know that he will make me proud someday.

My third child is very unique. He looked like an old man when he was born. He was born with a mustache and sideburns. He never really smiled as a baby and he was always so serious. He always studied everything around him and he was very quiet. As a baby, he always had a complex look on his face like he knew everything already. I knew he would be here before I even thought about getting pregnant.

I had a strange dream before I got pregnant. In my dream, I saw God. I know that sounds crazy but God said to me in my dream that I was chosen to give birth to a man child. Yes, I know it sounds crazy! I wasn't even having sex at the time. I was celibate for two years after I had Jahjah and I had written men off entirely. A couple of months after having the dream, I met his father. A couple of months after that is when I became pregnant.

I was by myself throughout the pregnancy and I was severely depressed because his father was denying him. Although I could have aborted him, I refused because I couldn't commit murder. I had done that before and I felt guilty for about a year after I had an abortion. I had gotten really sick because they left something inside of me that caused an infection and I vowed to never do that again!

While I was pregnant with him I had another dream, but this time it was about an angel. The angel said to me that God told him to tell me to give my son his name. I had already picked a name for him but because of the dream, I gave him both names—the name I chose, and the name that I dreamt of. I'm not sure why I had those dreams but I do know that I had them for a reason. Pooty is six years old and he is very sensitive. He is a mama's boy which is the complete opposite of Jahjah. Jah enjoys his space but Pooty enjoys my space. He loves to sneak in the bed with me while I'm sleeping and then I wake up to find him right next to me. He follows me around and he gets very sad when he is away from me for more than a day.

Pooty made me want to go back to school. I figured I had three children and nothing to offer them. I decided to go to college and further my education after I had him. I took some classes on campus and some online. I was determined to finish. I'm very happy that I made that decision because it changed my life for the better. Pooty is the side of me that is complex. He is the serious side. That is a side one rarely sees because I'm such a jokester. When I'm serious, it's because I need to be, not because I have to be. I see that in him everyday. I love him so much and I know that he will keep the other children grounded. He is not the type to get overly excited about anything unless he is in a very good mood.

My fourth child, Nini, is a big goof ball. She is never serious but she has quite a mean streak when she wants to be mean. I guarantee that no one will ever take advantage of her because she wouldn't let them. She is very soft spoken so people tend to take to her very quickly. They love her energy and her pretty light brown eyes. She is a daddy's girl, 100 percent, and she always finds a way to make me laugh because she is always doing something goofy. She doesn't like to see anyone hurt her brothers and sisters, and she gets very upset if you even yell at her daddy. If her siblings are fighting, she will cry because she hates violence. When the children play-fight with other children, she thinks that they're serious and she jumps right in!

She will never let any of her siblings get hurt and she is very protective of her younger sister especially. One time I was playing with the baby, and the baby started crying. Nini got very upset with me. She yelled at me and told me to stop hurting her sister, and then she hit me. I had to explain to her that I was only playing, but she was so upset with me that day. She is the part of me that jokes around. I see that in her. She loves to make others laugh just like me, and she doesn't know when to stop; just like I used to do when I was younger.

I got married for the second time when I was pregnant with her. After I had her, I realized that I was putting up with too much bull crap from men. I had four children and was basically a single parent even though I was married. It broke my heart, but I woke up one day and said to myself that I may not be Ms. America, but I sure deserve to be treated like that or better. I deserve to be with someone who is not going to cheat on me, who respects me, who is honest, who loves me and my children, who wouldn't beat on me, and who cares about me and my feelings. I vowed that I would never ever again settle. I have been by myself for about two years now and I enjoy it. I'm again practicing abstinence. I need to be happy and healthy so that I can take care of my beautiful family!

I cannot afford to contract any sexually transmitted diseases and I most certainly don't want to go through an emotional roller coaster. I feel that it would be wise to focus on raising my children and building a life for us so that we will never have to depend on another human being as long as I live. When I'm done getting to where I need to be in life, then I may focus on a relationship, but I doubt it. I'm in no rush to start dating again.

She made me wiser and stronger. I thank God that he sent me a brown-eyed angel. I don't know what I would do without either of them.

My fifth child is my little Pooda. She is definitely heaven sent. She has a smile that would light up any room and her dimples make it hard for me to say no to her. Out of all of my children; she is the one that I cannot say no to. When I do say no to the baby, I feel like the world is crashing down on me and I totally give in. She has the cutest personality. She gives me this look that is too cute to describe. Everyone that comes around her cannot help but fall into her charm. She melts hearts everywhere we go. She is too cute.

She craves attention and if all eyes are not on the little celebrity, she demands attention by doing something so darn cute. Her eyes are mesmerizing and her little fat cheeks make you want to just pinch them. She enjoys her independence and at the same time she is a mama's girl. She follows me from room to room and always wants my attention. Yet, she hates my kisses! If anyone tries to give her a kiss, she turns her head so quickly that you feel pretty stupid. Then she will gaze at you in such a way that you just have to laugh. She loves to do anything cute that will make you laugh.

Though she is the opposite from Nini because she is not generous at all, she is just like her in the sense that she is very protective of her siblings and me. I was just the same way when I was a child. Every time my grandfather came over or whenever we were around any family members, I would spontaneously perform, because I loved attention. I guess that is why I was in so many plays during school. I loved to perform and adored the attention. I'm almost certain she will be a celebrity of some sort.

She brings me joy, and no matter how down or angry I am, she finds a way to make me smile or feel better. I see it this way—you only live once and you can't spend your time obsessing over things that you can't fix.

I enjoy all five of my children, and their personalities. I can see bits and pieces of me in all of them. I don't need a man to complete me or my family because my children complete me. We are a real family, a loving family, and a happy family! I have my ups and my downs, but we all get through it and we stick together!

# Chapter 8: Wake Up

## Wake up

**November 15, 2007**

*Wake up my sisters, wake up.*
*Stop hiding behind weaves and make-up.*
*Learn to love the skin you're in,*
*Because your beauty comes from within.*
*Stop letting these men break you down.*
*Don't give them your throne and your crown.*
*Men will break your spirit and devour your soul,*
*Feed off of your love until he reaches his goal.*
*He will tell you he loves you and create a light,*
*Then leave you in a shadow of darkness with your heart cut out from his deceptive knife,*
*Make a child with you and deny his seed,*
*Leaving you to become mommy and daddy while he prays on his next victim's love to feed,*
*Wake up, my sisters, wake up,*
*You don't have to give up.*
*There is more to life then this.*
*Your child is not your burden; but your gift*
*Don't punish yourself or call your gift a mistake.*
*Your mistake was a lack of self-love and receptive heartache.*
*Dealing with his shit because you thought it was out of love.*
*Meanwhile he is with the next person and you're not even thought of.*
*Wake up, my sisters, wake up.*
*Stop oppressing yourselves and giving it up.*
*Your private life is your treasure.*
*It is of value to give someone who loves you unconditionally the pleasure.*

*Love yourself even if no one else loves you.*
*Self-love is the purest love; a love that's true.*
*When you love you, you will know how valuable that you are.*
*You are priceless—a rare gem that's brighter than any star.*
*You shine, baby girl; you shine so bright.*
*And when you are ready, God will send you someone who is right.*
*Wake up, my sisters, wake up.*
*Life's not over just because you break up.*
*There is so much more to life than unrequited love and no trust.*
*No matter how much you change or love him, it will never be enough.*
*You can fix your hair, buy new clothes and perfume.*
*If a man does not treat you right; then your relationship is doomed.*
*Look good for you, treat yourself to something nice.*
*You only live once, not twice.*
*Live everyday as if it was your last.*
*You're not promised tomorrow; live in the present and not the past.*
*Respect you, love you, and tell yourself that you are beautiful.*
*Wake up, my sisters, wake up.*
*It is time to resolve inner conflicts and stop letting these men use you!*

# Deceptive Plan

**December 8, 2007**

*I don't have any friends in my life.*
*I've been infected with pain and greeted with strife.*
*My health is fading, and tears, I have many.*
*Taken advantage of by others, adding stress by the penny,*
*Inhaling their lies as they speak.*
*Truthfully I'm stronger than they think as "I play the role" of the weak.*
*Come into my home with smiles covering their deceit.*
*Passive aggressive bullshit, but it is them I defeat.*
*Mindful of their plans to perform wicked deeds,*
*Playing the damsels in distress among flowers, but they're weeds.*
*Handing out excuses to make their plea*
*Hoping I fall for their schemes, I'll play as dumb as I could be.*
*Unfortunately, I give in, feeling sorry for the meek.*
*Don't be fooled by kindness, just because I don't speak.*
*I have God on my side, and he does not like ugly.*
*I will leave it all in his hands because they will reap what they sow when*
*they try to harm me.*
*For all of those who have taken advantage of someone giving a helping hand,*
*Shame on you and your deceptive plan!*

I have added this entry because I want those who chose to play on others' kindness to wake up! Some of those people who may be kind are only kind because they feel sorry for you. Some may be naïve and not even know that they're being used. I know when I'm being used, but I personally don't regret helping those who are in need. I only regret the fact that they're so greedy and needy. I hope to wake those people up who have thought that they were getting over someone and I'd like to tell them to get a life! Stop depending on others and start doing for yourself.

You are pitiful. How dare you take advantage of the very people who are there for you? The ones who could care less, you treated them well. Shame on you! Those who thought that they were putting something over on you FOOLED YOU! I only pitied you! Such a shame that you would pick on someone you feel is weak and defenseless!

**God bless you all!**
ENOUGH SAID…UNTIL NEXT TIME!

# Exit
## Tomorrow

**December 10, 2007**

*Tomorrow there will be sunshine but today there is only rain.*
*Tomorrow I will be happy, because raindrops wash away the pain.*
*I will evaluate things today because tomorrow is a fresh start.*
*Never again will I regret all of the hurt within my heart.*
*I had to cry in order to gain a smile.*
*My spirit had to grow through the tribulations of my trial.*
*Tomorrow my sadness will be a thing of the past.*
*Today I can glance at it all through the looking glass.*
*A person can carry their burdens in their face.*
*Tomorrow all of the stress lines will be erased.*
*Today I'm aggravated by the mistakes I have made.*
*Tomorrow I will have realized I need to let go and those bad memories will begin to fade.*
*Today I'm only a woman learning to deal with the pressures of life.*
*Tomorrow I will laugh at it all; no more tensions too thick to cut with a knife.*
*Today I look at it as just another day.*
*Tomorrow I will live life to the fullest and not waste another minute in dismay.*
*Yes, it is all clear that I have wasted my time dwelling on things that have happened so long ago.*
*Tomorrow is another day, but what I have learned today is that those bad days I must let go!*

Thank You!

Isabella M.

P.S. To live in the past is a mistake that we all make because it only makes living in the present full of resentment. Our past and present pave the way for our future. Forgive, but never forget! You will heal internally and it will show externally. Live, learn, let it go, move on, and you shall be free to live your life without regret!

# About the Author

A single mother of five who has endured physical, sexual, emotional, and mental abuse from the time that she was born from her mother. From being thrown into walls while only a few weeks old because she would not stop crying, to being starved for several days at a time as a severe punishment. She had a story to tell and her outlet was through her poetry. One day, she took a good look at her life and realized her strengths, took that strength to utilize it to empower and uplift herself and others. Through her struggles, pain and cry for help, she contemplated suicide many times. Her depression pushed her over the edge until one morning she woke up and realized that time was passing by and she devalued her life because she gave her power to her oppressors. Her pain gave her strength, and her courage gave her a reason to live and help others in her situation. She took that and decided that she was someone of value, and realizing her degree of worth she finished school and decided to take her talents and utilize it in order to defeat her past and empower her future. Now she uses her strengths to help others who have been through or are going through similar struggles and she will continue until her last breath. Isabella M. is a talented poet who looks at life from a different prespective, and though some of her poetry has sort of an meloncholy tone, most can relate somehow with a story of their own.

Printed in the United States
121233LV00009B/121/P

729-5025